LEADERSHIP
IN THREE WORDS

The Art and Science of
Educational Leadership

Michelle McQueen-Williams, Ph.D.

DEDICATED TO...

The God of my salvation.
I give Him all honor and praise, for without Him, I would not
have had such a wonderful career in education, my life's work.
To God be the glory for the great things He has done!

My son, Byron Williams,
who grew up with a mom who was trying to lead
while loving him unconditionally.

My family, especially my mother and father,
Tyrone and Ella McQueen,
who supported my every educational endeavor.

The mentors and colleagues
who have traveled this leadership journey
ahead and alongside me.

The principals and teachers
who do the tough work of leading schools and
the children who benefit because of that leadership.

TABLE OF CONTENTS

My leadership identity was established and my dream realized after being featured in an article entitled "Building Effective School Leaders." I was featured for being named the planning principal at Harvie Elementary School, the newest elementary school in Eastern Henrico, Virginia.

INTRODUCTION

After 30 years in public education, my phone hasn't stopped ringing yet! I'm not complaining. I love people, listening to their stories, and helping them overcome their challenges by offering a sound word of advice whenever I can. Most of the phone calls I receive are from education professionals, of course, because that is the field in which I served for the entirety of my career. Sometimes, they want advice about how to handle a leadership matter. Other times, they just want me to listen; they already know what they want to do or how they should proceed and simply want validation. In such cases, I always give my two cents, and then I end with, "Whatever you decide, you have to own it!" In other words, whether their decision is right or wrong, as long as they make it from the heart and not out of an intent to harm, and as long as they are willing to assume final responsibility for what happens, I stand behind them.

What people like most about me is that I have mastered the art of giving advice without giving instructions. For example, when people ask me, "What do you think about this?" I respond by asking them, "What do you think about it?" I never really give them the answer; I just listen, explain the principle that is at play, give them advice (if they ask me for it), and let them make their own informed decisions.

Regardless of the situation, however, people who call me know that I'm not going to give them the "politically correct" perspective and advice; I'm going to be real with them and tell them the truth. I've been living long enough to know that everyone is not going to tell you exactly how they feel about things; they tell you things that are safe. I understand that, too. Sometimes, you have to play it safe, and other times, you have to shoot straight. I'll admit that most of the time, I'm a straight shooter. I'm not afraid to say unpopular things or have tough conversations, so I embrace them head-on. I do so because I have a conscience; I want to be able to sleep at night knowing that the advice or guidance I gave came from a truthful and honest place that was motivated by a sincere desire to help and not to hinder. When giving advice in general, I recognize that I'm dealing with people's lives. Even more is at stake with educational leaders that I counsel and advise, because children's lives are at stake. It's way bigger than us.

People who have worked with me over the years will tell you, "Dr. McQueen is not going to tell you anything that she wouldn't do herself." I'm also not going to give you advice on something that I know nothing about. Those who come to me do so because they have confidence in me to lay things out and make things plain based on my training and experiences. I'm going to be honest with them; I will tell them if I agree or disagree or if there is a meeting in the middle. I don't talk to them just to talk to them; I talk *with* them so I can be of help. I say, "Let's talk together!" Then, I get into the trenches with them. If they are fired up, I'm going to get fired up right along with them. If they are in an emotionally-difficult place, I'm going to show compassion and empathize with them right where they are.

Perhaps you're wondering, *Why are you telling us all of this, Dr. McQueen?* I'm glad you asked! I share these things with you so that you will understand where I'm coming from, my motivation for penning this book. I've been asked over and over again why I haven't written a book that encapsulates all of my years of experience and what many refer to as my "sage advice" on all things dealing with education and leadership. Well, in my semi-retirement from public education, I finally have the time – as well as countless lessons to share under my belt. I wrote this book not out of vanity but out of demand. So many leaders in education are in a place where they desperately need advice and really don't have anyone to turn to who will give it to them in a transparent, straightforward, non-politically correct way. That's where I come into the picture. Allow me, my years of experience, and the wisdom that I have gained from my education career to help!

Leading schools is tough work. I know this for a fact. I have worn a lot of hats along my career in educational leadership. I have served as a high school assistant principal. I have served as a turnaround principal in an elementary school, opened up an elementary school with the help of a great team, and served as a director of elementary schools. The toughest leadership challenge was when I was asked to lead a school that had not met state standards and given the keys to the school three days before teachers returned. That year, the school was in the 50th percentile. The following year, through leadership and a committed team, it was fully accredited. As director of elementary schools, one of my responsibilities was supervising principals. Some of them were leading schools that had failed to meet accreditation requirements. Working together, their schools became accredited, too. Of course, people ask me all the time how to turn challenged schools into high-performing schools in a short time. My response is always the same: by keeping the main thing the main thing. What's the main thing? What's best for the students. It's always about the students.

Each of these positions came with its own unique set of difficult challenges and obstacles, so when I say that my experiences have run the gamut of tough work in education, I mean it. Working in education has really been a trial by fire! Fortunately, I've learned some valuable lessons along the way, and I'm really good at teaching them to other people.

Throughout my career, I've poured my heart into my work and invested countless hours, time and energy into ensuring that the students had access to the best education possible so they could have the best future possible. Every decision I made, initiative I implemented, program I developed, and challenge that I placed on my staff and teachers were about the students – the main thing.

These principles I present on the pages of this book are designed to help you keep the main thing the main thing, and the only way to do this is to remember why it is you originally signed up for the work. If I had to take a guess, I know why you signed up for a career in education: it's because you cared, and you want to make a difference. This has consistently been my experience with men and women working in education whom I've encountered over the years. Out of curiosity, I ask them why they became a teacher, principal or administrator, and I can almost predict their response word for word. They were impacted by a teacher, counselor or principal who really cared about them and invested in them years ago, and it made them want to be an educator. They see working in education as a way to shape the minds and futures of the next generation, and since they care so much about young people, they wanted to be a part of this significant work. Does this sound like you? If so, that's awesome. I applaud your selflessness and your heart for wanting to pour your life into these young people, who need it the most.

After working for so many years in education, I'm a good profiler – I can read people well, especially educators. For example, if you're a teacher or aspiring teacher, there's a strong likelihood that in addition to wanting to make a difference, you are also a planner, organized and resilient, but you're also stressed out, are under a great deal of pressure, and feel consumed or overwhelmed by your job. If you're an administrator, you fit the same profile, but you're also quite likely to be competitive, data driven – and fearful. You fear failure. You fear that your professional image is at stake because it is based on your performance. You fear that your reputation in the school system would be blemished if you fail at leading your school.

Regardless of what level of educational leader you are, whether teacher, assistant principal, principal, or district administrator, I know that you are likely to possess the most important trait in the profile: you love it. You love the students. You love the education community, the relationships, the families you serve, the collaboration, camaraderie, and team-oriented environment... you love it all.

However, this doesn't mean that things don't get hard sometimes. In fact, I know from experience that things can get so difficult and overwhelming sometimes that despite all the love you have for education, you actually consider quitting. As much as you've studied, taken tests, gone to trainings and invested countless effort into building your education career, it can become so much that you don't feel that you can go on for another year. You start fantasizing about what life would be like without the early mornings and late evenings of preparation, without having to take your work home with you, without the pressure to ensure that your students perform and that you perform effectively as a leader – an easier, less-stressful life. You even begin tossing around the idea of being a stay-at-home mom, starting your own small business, or working in the corporate world. Then, you come to yourself and you say, "I can't quit... I love working in education and my students, and I don't want to do anything else!" I understand.

We all reach these low points sometimes. However, when we are in such a state, it's hard to be an effective leader. Leadership effectiveness takes being in a zone in which you are hopeful, optimistic and filled with positive energy. How can you get back into this zone? The book you're reading is the first step. You need some inspiration, and I'm here to give it to you. However, I'm not just going to inspire you with positive words that tell you, "You're a winner!" I'm going to inspire you by empowering you with principles and teaching you practices that are so easy to implement, they're going to increase your confidence and make you feel you're capable of getting them done. You'll feel inspired simply because you'll be able to see your way to being more effective!

As an educator, you've learned a lot of educational leadership theory in the classroom and at seminars, trainings and workshops. I wrote this book to take you beyond theory and allow you to benefit from the practical lessons learned throughout my decades of experience at every level of educational leadership. I want you to walk away from reading this book with essential keys and everyday principles you can immediately use on the job as you strive to become the most effective leader possible.

I like to say that I wrote this book for you because it is the book that I needed and wish I'd had myself when I was an ambitious

30-year-old, just beginning my brand new administrative career in education. I needed someone to take me aside and give me some practical advice about the things that weren't covered in the classroom. I needed some real-life advice and insights on how to overcome leadership challenges and succeed as an educational leader.

However, this book is not only for those who are new to educational leadership or administration; it also offers myriad benefits for those who have been leaders in education for decades. Maybe you've been a leader in the same building forever without being able to shift things or produce any change, so you've lost some of your hopefulness, optimism and enthusiasm for leadership. Even worse, maybe your school is failing, and you simply don't know what to do about it. Perhaps you're feeling stuck in a place you really don't want to be anymore, or burnout, and all you want is to feel motivated again, reigniting the passion you once had that got you into the work and made you love going to work every day. Or, you might still be enthusiastic about the work, but you feel ineffective as a leader because despite all your best efforts, you just can't seem to make the school work the way you want it to work. Then, you might fall into the category where you don't feel anything anymore; you're apathetic. You're just going through the motions day in and day out and surviving the best you can.

If any of these scenarios describes you, don't worry. You might just need a shot in the arm to get your "mojo" back, and this book can give it to you. The practical keys and principles that I offer will give you the opportunity to learn fresh ways of looking at various leadership challenges so you can approach them with a new sense of enthusiasm. It will inspire you by helping to build in you the hopefulness, motivation, courage, and sense of efficacy you need to keep going and realize your goal of greater leadership effectiveness. It's my job to help you be more fearless and less timid, ready and equipped to step your game up and be as effective as possible. I want to inspire you to the point that you throw your hands into the air, throw your head back, and shout, "I can do this!" from the top of your lungs. You're right: you can do this tough work, and I'm going to help you do it.

As you are being inspired by the lessons I am imparting, take special note of what I call "Queenisms." Everyone who has ever worked with me knows that I have Queenisms, which are unique quotes and sayings that I have crafted throughout my career. They represent the principles for which I stand as an educational leader – my leadership philosophy. These Queenisms have served me well over the years and were fundamental to my leadership effectiveness. Feel free to adopt them as your own!

Most of all, as we go on this journey to greater leadership effectiveness, I want for us to have fun! There's nothing like being in dry, boring environments; they will zap all of the energy and enthusiasm out of you! To me, the best learning environments are those that blend substance, practicality, and fun, and that is exactly the atmosphere I aim to create through the pages of this book. Let's laugh a little! When you're immersed in the responsibilities of leadership, especially when the pressure is on you to get clear, measurable results, things can get pretty serious. You deserve to let off a little steam and have a chuckle or two at yourself and at others who are in the same boat, doing everything possible to hold everything together on the outside but on the verge of running out the front doors of your school and down the street yelling, "They can have the darn school!" on the inside. You need a break. Let's take one together by having a little fun. It is possible to get empowered, be inspired, learn to be a more effective leader and enjoy yourself along the way. Leadership matters, so let's get it done!

1

THIS IS HEARTWORK

I'm a "real talk" kind of person. I'll just go ahead and say the things that other people dance around and won't come out and say, because I believe that openness is the best approach... especially when it comes to meeting the needs of students. That said, I think it's essential that we talk about motivation in education. Over the years, I have identified three things that tend to motivate the work of leaders in education: the head, the ego, and the heart. Work that is motivated by the head will get things done but leave people feeling like you don't care, and care is important in an education environment. Work motivated by the ego might get things done but will produce an atmosphere in which people do not support you; they might even try to sabotage you. Work motivated by the heart will make people feel like you care for them, and because of this, you will do the hard work that is best for your stakeholders. When you allow the heart to motivate your work, everyone wins.

The unfortunate reality is that I've seen many leaders motivated by the ego, and their outcomes reflect this. Although I've seen the ego at work at every level of leadership, it tends to be most prominent among administrative leaders. They love being in charge and in control. They love coming to work every day and seeing their name on the door. They love the power and influence that comes along with having a high-level position. Most of all, they love how the people in the environment they lead acquiesce to them, cater to their desires, and go out of their way to please them. If you are a leader in the field, you can be honest: you know someone who operates that way, too. The problem is that if you are not careful, these things can feed your sense of self to the point that you begin to feel a little too important – like the most important person in the education environment. This can be dangerous to one's leadership effectiveness.

Don't get me wrong: we all have an ego. If you say you don't, you are not being honest. However, it should not motivate the work of leaders in education. Education is a world that is centered not on what is best for one's ego but always on what is best for the students – your primary stakeholders. Everything should revolve around them and their best interests, not around the leader who sees him or herself as the center of the education universe! Many times, doing what is best for the students will come at the cost of the leader's ego, so it is important that leaders understand when their work is being motivated by their ego.

Then, there are leaders who allow their head to motivate their work. They are typically driven by things like intellect and programmatic rationale – things that make the most sense on paper. They are all about information and checklists, and they're all about getting things done to make themselves and whatever they are leading look good in the data. Leaders who are motivated by head work tend to be focused on checking off all of their milestones, meeting all of their benchmarks, meeting, planning, organizing, and turning in all of their reports on time. Building relationships with their stakeholders, keeping tabs on how the people in the environment feel, and creating a culture of togetherness, camaraderie, and oneness are not their priorities. They are laser focused on performance. Again, head work is not a bad thing. Head work keeps the educational environment functioning smoothly and operating according to state regulations, so there's no need to shake your head at it! However, an educational leader's primary motivation in leading should not be head; it should be heart. You might say, "No, Dr. McQueen, that's where you're wrong. The head should be primary. It's the most important part of a leader's work!" However, I'm going to challenge you on this. My position is that leading schools does indeed require "head" work, or intellect and rationale, but ultimately, this is heartwork.

QUEENISM

When you change the language, you change the culture!

Education work is Heartwork because you have to feel something if you are going to work with people, especially in an education setting. You've got to be able to feel what they are going through and sense where they are coming from in order to adequately address their needs as a leader, and you can't do any of this without a heart – the ability to sense and feel. People's lives are on the line. They are more than figures, statistics, and cases to be driven through a machine or a system; they are actual living, breathing human beings who have hearts, feelings and stories of their own, and you must be able to relate to them as such. You will never be effective as a leader with them without being able to connect with them in your heart.

I know that some of you might not naturally be "feelers." You're likely more of a "head work" type of person that prefers focusing on computer screens, compiling data, planning programs, and writing reports. You're all about the execution of the plan, not the building of relationships, because you're more of a thinker than a feeler. I've got good news: there's hope for you. I've worked with people like you many, many times, and I happen to know that you *can* be effective in building relationships with your stakeholders; it's just going to take some extra-intentional effort on your part to do so. If you desire to become a more effective leader through building relationships – doing the Heartwork – you will succeed if you view it positively. By "positively," I mean viewing regarding Heartwork as being more important than head work and as something that is attainable rather than impossible. If you're a "heady" person and you have absolutely no desire to even *try* to engage in Heartwork, what can I say? You might be in the wrong business.

Like many educators, I initially got into the business of education because of the heart: I had a passionate desire to play a part in shaping the futures of children and youth. I enjoyed being a teacher, connecting with my students, and seeing their growth and transformation each year. It was deeply fulfilling work! One day, about two or three years into my teaching career, the superintendent was at my school. I was in the hallway interacting with some students, who were not my own. I kept telling them that they needed to get to class but they preferred to keep hanging out with and talking to me. Eventually, they went their way, but not before the superintendent observed me and my interaction with the students. Later, I would find out that the superintendent had asked my principal who I was, and my principal told him. Then, he shared with my principal that the district was about to form a new leadership cohort and sent me some information about participating. From there, the rest was history. I would go on to complete the leadership program and then move to administrative leadership. What did the superintendent see in me? I don't know for certain, but I do have an idea: he saw my heart for the students that I was interacting with, and he saw that I was loving, but also had expectations for students to go to class.

Just as I believe the superintendent saw my heart for the students, others can see your heart as a leader – or lack thereof. So can I. It doesn't take me long to tell whether someone is in it for something other than the kids. During my years in educational leadership, I always emphasized to those under my leadership that we don't lead for the pocket, prestige or power. As I always used to say, "You're not going to make a paycheck on the backs of these kids!" In other words, if someone isn't doing what they are supposed to be doing to serve the best interests of the students, they don't deserve to work in an education environment. If they are in their position to get more money (pocket), to gain more notoriety or influence (prestige), or to wield authority over people (power), they are operating from a self-serving position. In fact, it's from the position of the ego. They will never be effective as they could be as leaders, because the most effective leaders focus on serving others, not serving themselves.

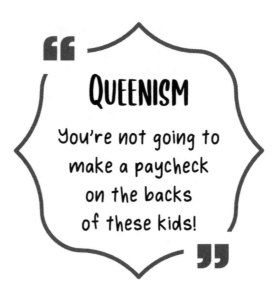

QUEENISM

You're not going to
make a paycheck
on the backs
of these kids!

Your students are the primary ones but not the only ones that you must have a heart for when you are involved in educational leadership. You've also got to be able to connect to and serve the interests of everyone from the teachers and parents to the cafeteria workers and the custodians. Your heart can't be connected to the students without consideration for those who help to create a clean, comfortable and safe learning environment for them day in and day out. What about the guys making $10 an hour pushing the floor mop so kids can have a clean place to learn? You need to deal with them from the heart. What about the paraprofessionals who often get overlooked because they are not "real teachers"? They are vital to the learning environment and you should deal with them from the heart, too. Dealing with the heart simply means treating them like real people and showing them the same courtesy, care and concern that you share with others who are deemed "more important."

For example, when I was a principal and we celebrated Teacher Appreciation Day, I always made sure that we invited the paraprofessionals. When we had appreciation days, I included all of the staff at the school, including the cafeteria workers. Also, as I was planning appreciations for my staff in the school, I made sure that I didn't forget the custodial staff. These are often the most underpaid and underappreciated staff members in the school house, even though they play such an instrumental role in the school. They keep the building clean and ensure students can learn in an inviting environment, which is essential in helping the school to accomplish its bottom line of delivering a quality education to the students. In recognition of their importance, and out of a genuine heartfelt relationship with them, every Christmas, I would give gifts to my custodial staff. One Christmas, I gave all of my custodians leather jackets. You would have thought I had given them each a million dollars! Another Christmas, I gave each of the custodians little portable televisions. I also made it a habit to eat lunch with them once a week, which is not something that most principals do. Pretty soon, my custodians would brag to custodians at other schools, so word got around to other schools that Dr. McQueen really took care of her custodians! In light of this, I had to be sure to "go big or go home" every year. I gladly did so, because it was Heartwork for me. I can recall leaving one school and going to work at another school, and I took one of my custodians with me. He would report back to the first school all that I would do to take care of my custodial staff, build a relationship with them, and make them feel appreciated. He told them about all of the nice things that they had received from me; he was trying to make the other custodians jealous. When I eventually left that school, this same custodian shared with my successor, "You need to make sure you appreciate your custodial staff!" Of course, I received a call from that principal! All schools have a discretionary fund that building leaders can use for whatever needs their school might have, at their discretion. I chose to use a part of my budget to appreciate my staff in a way that made a huge impact on them.

I encouraged that principal to do the same, because he did have the choice to do so!

Did I have to do these things? No. I chose to do them from the heart. I chose to see them as people who had value, not as insignificant things to be cast aside and forgotten. As a result, I gained even greater leadership influence with them, which contributed to my effectiveness. They would be so eager to do anything for me that I asked! Ultimately, it takes a *whole stakeholder body* to make a school run smoothly – not just a principal, assistant principals, office staff, and teachers – so you should make an attempt to connect with every one of them from the heart.

Whenever I talk about education being Heartwork, I have to be sure to strike a balance. What I don't want you to walk away thinking is that every decision you make and action you take when leading an education environment should be driven by feelings, relationships, and your connections with people – the heart. While most of your motivation for your decisions and actions should begin with the heart, there are also those that must include the head. This should be something that goes without saying to an educational leader, but it's always better to over-clarify than let people walk away unclear about what I mean.

One of the best examples that I can offer that shows the balance in the head and the heart is when you're sitting in a room with your team reviewing assessment data. Let's say that 60% of the students passed the assessment, but 40% of the students did not pass. Typically, the people around the table looking at the report will focus on the 40% that did not pass. They'll keep saying, "This is what we need to do with the 40%," or "The 40% needs to participate in a remediation program." They'll continue talking about the 40% like these students are numbers – head work – rather than living, breathing individual souls – Heartwork. Each of them represents a story, and if we only relate to them as statistics and numbers, we'll never do what's necessary to understand them as individual human beings.

I'll say to the team, "Help me understand why you are just focusing on this 40% of students who did not pass the assessment as a collective entity. Let's see who they are. What's their story? What have they missed? What individualized remediation does each student need to get up to speed?" I challenge them to deal with the kids as individuals, not numbers. Yes, numbers tell the truth, but the truth is still wrapped up in a "somebody." Numbers are the truth about what is happening, but there are still reasons that the truth is the truth for that kid, and these reasons need to be investigated. For example, did the kid have a fight on the bus before the assessment? Did his parents have an argument before school? Did the kid come in late to school? Did he miss breakfast and go to class hungry? All of these things can affect a child and leave him mentally unprepared to do the work or pass the assessment. You have to ask questions about each individual case when you are presented with the data. You need to drill down to investigate the who, what and why behind the numbers. This is the Heartwork that helps you to become a more effective leader.

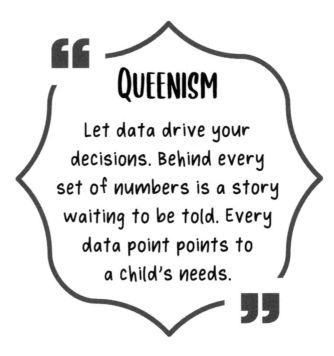

QUEENISM

Let data drive your decisions. Behind every set of numbers is a story waiting to be told. Every data point points to a child's needs.

Since I'm not a novice to educational leadership, I know that there are some who might inevitably say, "Dr. McQueen, I get that this is 'Heartwork,' but leading with the heart just isn't realistic in the kind of school I lead. It's a rough school with rough stakeholders, and leading with the heart will cause me to get run over by everyone!" I disagree. I know from experience that it can be done! Leading with the heart simply means that you actually care and are concerned about the stakeholders you serve as a leader – and you show it. Caring and concern are things that you can demonstrate to people of any class or background. Everyone, regardless of socioeconomic status (SES), likes to know that their leader cares about them! Again, not only does leading from this perspective transform the way that you lead, but it makes you more effective with the people you lead by giving you more influence with them.

In low-SES schools, poverty is not the issue; it's your response to the poverty that makes the difference. For example, when you're leading in a school context like this, the Heartwork consists of things like making sure the kids have food and snacks, frequently holding motivational and awards assemblies, ensuring that you have face time with the kids, doing home visits, and making them feel like you and your team want them at school (and yes, kids *can* feel this!). As a leader in a low-SES school, all you can control is six hours in the students' day; you can't control what happens after they leave, but you can make a huge difference in their lives while they are in your building and under your leadership. While they are in your building and under your care, you do the Heartwork when you make sure they are loved, that they know they matter, that they are fed and clothed. These "wrap-around services" are all a part of the Heartwork – the "extra" that is necessary in these contexts to ensure that the kids can focus on learning and getting a quality education.

I know that doing the Heartwork can make a difference in a low-SES school from experience. When I arrived as the principal of Glen Lea Elementary School in 2001, they had the second-lowest scores in the division in terms of student performance. By the time I left in 2008, we were ranked in the middle, and this was in comparison to high-SES schools. We had a 75% poverty rate, but because my team and I did the Heartwork, our kids were performing well above the level at which the community thought they could perform. However, our students' performance didn't surprise me; I was undaunted by their low-SES context and knew that leading from the heart could impact any educational environment. Some educators would not even want to set foot into a low-SES school because of the challenges they know they would face. In fact, some educators have an invisible asterisk on their resume that indicates *I want this kind of position but only in a high-SES school or district,* because they don't want to put in the "extra" that comes from leading in a low-SES. What they do not realize is that regardless of whether a school is a high-SES school or a low-SES school, there will be challenges. For example, in a high-SES school, you might have to deal with the challenge of helicopter parents, while in a lower-SES school, you will have to deal with children coming to school hungry. Every school is going to have challenges and addressing these challenges will require doing the Heartwork. There's no escaping it! When you embrace the challenge to lead from the heart, you will be a more effective leader in whatever education context you lead.

Just as most educators won't come out and say, "I don't want to work with poor kids because they have too many problems," there are other things that they will not say but that I know to be true about Heartwork. One of the biggest things that most will not dare to say aloud is that they believe that kids should just come equipped to want to come to school, go to class, learn, do homework, etc. However, many kids, particularly those in low-SES schools, do not come equipped from the home; the school leaders must do the Heartwork to motivate the kids to embrace all that school has to offer. Whatever they will do well, they will do well because it was something the school leaders promoted, incentivized, recognized, and rewarded. This Heartwork inspires the students and makes them want to repeat the same behaviors all over again. Think about it: even as an adult, you love getting rewards. When you do well on your job, you get a bonus or a raise, and this makes you feel good. If you get rewarded at work for doing what you are "already supposed to do," why shouldn't kids get rewarded for what they are "supposed to do"? Heartwork matters regardless of who you are and what you're doing. Just as it has an impact on you, it will have an impact on the stakeholders you lead in the education environment.

Remember when I said at the beginning of the book that I was writing not only to new educational leaders but to those who have been working in education for decades? One of the things that I know for sure is that the longer you work in a challenging field – and as quiet as it's kept, education is a *very* challenging field – the more likely it is that you'll begin to suffer burnout over time. Part of this burnout can include losing your heart for the people in the education environment. You started out great – you loved, connected with, showed care and concern for, and really invested yourself in the lives of your stakeholders. However, this might have taken a toll on you over the years. You might be at a point where you've grown tired of giving so much of yourself to others and feel depleted, like you don't have what it takes mentally and emotionally to continue doing this Heartwork anymore. I'll admit it: Heartwork does cost the leader a lot... but it's worth it. It pays off in increased leadership effectiveness. My advice is not to count yourself out quite yet. Try pouring back into yourself – prioritizing some "me" time – before you make a decision to quit. I recommend getting a journal and writing down your thoughts and emotions, going to the gym, taking a mini vacation to a spa for some pampering, or stepping away for a weekend and spending time with your family. Everyone is different and is at different levels of mental and emotional depletion, so do whatever replenishes you the most. For some, it will take more than others to regain the heart you once had for leading in an education environment. When I was a principal, I could get replenished and stave off burnout simply by going outside to the playground and playing with the kids. Other times, I would go outside to the school's athletic field and walk on the track while the kids were running. These school breaks might not seem like much, but they were my way of getting things off of my mind and pouring back into myself. They were my way of ensuring that I could continue the Heartwork necessary for being an effective leader.

If you do not already do so, embrace the reality that education is not only "hard work"; it is "Heartwork." Operating from this position is sure to give you a greater connection to your stake-holders, increase your influence with them, and increase your effectiveness as a leader.

(2)
PEOPLE BEFORE PAPER

I like to say, "Being an educational leader consists of both paperwork and people work." However, people come before paper, because as educators, we are in the people business, not the paper business. When you embrace that you are in the people business, it helps to realign your priorities, and consequently, your daily decisions and activities. You spend more time listening to people, gathering ideas, collaborating with all of your stakeholders, and being present and visible. When you operate from a position of being in the paper business, you immerse yourself in analyzing data, filling out papers, creating reports, etc., all of which reduces your engagement with the people you serve as a leader.

If you're not careful and deliberate, paperwork will become all-consuming and swallow up every bit of your time and attention. Every day you sit at your desk and open your email, you are going to be met with requests and requirements for more and more paperwork. If you've been an educational leader for more than a month or so, you know the truth of this: the paperwork never seems to end. Because of this, it is important that you embrace my second principle: people come before paper.

I have always had an open door policy in my office, literally and figuratively. It is literal because my door was physically almost always open. Seeing an open office door says to people, "Come in," while a closed door says, "Stay out!" It invites them to come and talk to me, and this is exactly what I want. My open door policy is figurative because I always try to be available to the people I lead, which are my stakeholders.

I want all of my stakeholders, whether principals, counselors, teachers, parents, and even students, that I serve to know that I'm always available to them. I want them to know that I accepted my leadership position, not because I wanted to close myself away in an office and spend my time shuffling papers or on a computer, but because I wanted to interface with the people. I became an educational leader because I wanted to serve my stakeholders, and serving them means being available to them when they needed me. What about you? Why did you become an educational leader?

When I try to encourage people to embrace my People Before Paper principle, someone will inevitably ask me the question, "How am I supposed to get all of my work done if people are always popping into my office?" The key to this is striking a balance (balance when implementing any of my principles is key) between getting the sea of required paperwork done and being there for the people. I followed an 80/20 rule: I spent 80% of my time engaging with people, talking to parents, talking to teachers, and making sure the kids were okay. Then, I spent 20% of my time doing administrative paperwork either early in the morning before people started arriving at the school, but most often, later in the day after the school day ended. This way, I ensured that I got my work done while keeping people my priority as a leader. Would I have to take some of my paperwork home on occasion to make sure it all got done? As a leader, you already know that the answer to this is yes; leaders in any industry have to take paperwork home at some point. However, doing paperwork before and after school and at home is a small price to pay for increasing your leadership effectiveness on the job because you've spent the bulk of your time prioritizing people.

Early mornings and late afternoons are rarely a surprise to those who become assistant principals or principals in a school or in district administration. Most of them started off as great teachers, and great teachers are all too familiar with arriving at school early and staying late after the school day ends to do their planning and paperwork. They learned to do this so that they could spend the lion's share of their day working with the kids. When they go up in the ranks to become assistant principals or principals, the same principle applies: use the bulk of the school day for the stakeholders and save the paperwork for later.

When you begin to prioritize the "people work" of being a school leader, you'll realize that just as incessant as the paperwork can be, the people work, when done properly, can also be never ending. As a people-focused principal, I was always "out on those streets" (i.e., serving the people). I was either in the hallways interacting with students and asking them what they had learned or evaluating teachers, observing classroom instruction, talking to custodians and cafeteria workers, etc. As long as there were stakeholders on campus, there was always something to do – someone to serve. In between the busy times, I could run to my office real quick and return some phone calls, but this always came after the "face work" and engaging the people. If you want to be an effective educational leader, always remember:

the work is *not* in the office! The work is outside of the office as you serve the people!

The face work that comes when you prioritize People Before Paper can occur on several levels. I rank face work based on the following levels:

- **"Speaking"** – These are quick words of "Hello," "How's it going?" "Goodbye, and see you tomorrow," and "Take care!" that you use to greet stakeholders throughout the day. "Speaking" could also just be a nod, a thumbs up, a smile, and a wave or a wink. It's an acknowledgement of people to simply show them that you see them. This type of face work only takes a second or two and is usually done in passing. Even though it only takes a moment, it is important to your stakeholders that you speak, as it shows respect. Leaders who do not speak to their stakeholders can be considered stand-offish, high-minded, disconnected, uninterested, aloof, and poor leaders. Not taking the time to speak definitely hurts your leadership effectiveness.

- **"Shooting the breeze"** – This is an extended interaction with a stakeholder that can take a minute or two. The exchange is not about anything serious and usually involves individuals providing insight into their lives, including what they are planning to do that week or weekend, what's going on in their family, or what they have recently seen, heard or experienced. People appreciate when their leaders take the time to shoot the breeze with them. They perceive their leaders as down to earth, relatable, genuine, and someone who cares. "Shooting the breeze" is an important part of increasing your leadership effectiveness.

- **"Getting a minute"** – This level of face work takes a few minutes. It usually begins with someone either stopping you in the hallway, peeking their head into your office door, or pulling you aside in a classroom or the cafeteria and asking, "Can I get a minute?" By "a minute," people generally mean a few minutes. They don't plan to take much of your time; they just need to make you aware of something, get an answer to something, to get direction from you or to bring resolve to an issue. "Getting a minute" typically takes a little longer than "Shooting the breeze," but this type of face work is much shorter than the next level of face work, which is a more intensive conversation. When you allow people to pop in and "get a minute," wherever this occurs, you communicate to them that you are accessible as their leader and that you are not too busy to serve them. Plus, there's a bonus: the more "minutes" you give, the less people will have to come to your office when you're trying to do the paperwork that the job requires.

- **"Making an appointment"** – This is, by far, the most intensive level of face work. It occurs when a stakeholder needs more of your time and focus than a quick minute in the hallway or the classroom will allow. When you sense that a matter is serious to a stakeholder, you show that you recognize the seriousness of the matter by saying, "I'd really like to sit down and talk with you about this. Do you mind making an appointment to come in so we can give this matter the attention it deserves?" The request to meet with you in your office might also come from your stakeholders. Regardless of where the idea of "Making an appointment" so you can sit down and meet originates, it's important that you keep your schedule open enough to accommodate these requests. Never allow yourself to become so busy that you can't take appointments and address the matters that are of critical concern to your stakeholders.

Even though I've broken face work into four levels, I don't want you to become so rigid in your engagement with people that you make it harder than it is. When you are focused on doing Heartwork, these communications will naturally flow. For example, I can remember instances when I would be shooting the breeze with one of my school office staff members, and she would say something about having to leave work early on Friday because her son had a soccer game. Then, on Monday, I would circle back on this information that I learned while shooting the breeze and ask her how the soccer game went. That's people work – Heartwork – and it is gold! Also, I made sure to learn the names of my teams' children. Yes, it took a little while, but with some intentionality, I would ask them, "How are Evan and Micah doing?" This goes a lot further with stakeholders than simply asking, "How are the kids?" When I was a director of schools, there were four women in my schools who had babies. I learned all of the babies' names, and when the women returned to work, I asked about each baby by name. I can't tell you how much they appreciated this! Taking the time to learn the names of people's family members shows that you care. You might not actually really care at all, but the level of work that you put into your interactions with people will make them think you do, and that's what matters. It will still help to increase your leadership effectiveness.

As a school principal, I made it my business to be highly visible to the people I served. I wanted people not just to know my name and that I was the building leader, but I wanted them to actually see me leading. I also didn't want my stakeholders to view me as some mysterious, elusive figure who was so high up that I was untouchable or who was some prominent dignitary that was so important they had to be very special individuals to gain access to me. I was intentional about being both visible and accessible to my stakeholders, because I wanted them to know that we were all in this together. Most people already have a perception that being a principal is an ivory tower job where a disengaged school leader gets to tell people what to do, so your being visible to the people you serve helps to change this perception. Otherwise, your stakeholders will start to believe that they are out there on their own, and this will do nothing but decrease your leadership effectiveness. A visible leader is the kind of leader that people want, and this is the kind of leader that I encourage you to be.

As soon as I stepped into the school building every morning, I would sit at my office and have some "seat time," a time for devotion before people started arriving at the school. This time, which would last for about an hour or so, would be used to review my email and read and reply to only the most critical messages in my inbox. As soon as people started showing up, I would leave my office and immediately hit the hallways. Walking up and down each hallway, I would speak to every teacher, parent and student that I saw in the building. That was my most important job every day; not emails, not daily planning, not paperwork – just people. Further, I did not walk the hallways empty handed as I interacted with the people; I kept a trusty little notepad and pen with me so I could make notes of what my people needed and what I needed to do to support them, serve them, and meet their needs. As I interacted with students, if they told me they needed something, I wrote it down. As I interacted with teachers, if they told me they needed to leave early, that they didn't have enough work packets and needed help making some copies, etc. I wrote it down. Most importantly, I made sure to personally follow up on everything I wrote down on the notepad. Can you imagine how much that increased my influence and effectiveness with the people I served?

If you are going to be an effective leader, you need to make it a priority to be highly visible and touchable in the environment you lead. Believe me, no one likes an invisible leader. Invisible leaders are not relatable, and they can be out of touch with their stakeholders. Worst of all, when stakeholders have problems and issues that require your leadership intervention, they'll be less likely to reach out to you because they have already developed a schema about you that says you're inaccessible and untouchable. That's no good. I can tell you a lot of "horror stories" that I've encountered and heard about over the years that had as their central character a leader who was more comfortable doing paperwork than people work. As a director, I have worked with principals who were frequently in the office. Mind you, they weren't just hanging out; they were having meeting after meeting, and they were always working on some project or another. They were nearly invisible! Parents and teachers saw them as detached, disciplinary problems were at an all-time high because of low student interaction, and surveys evaluating performance came back negative from all stakeholders, because prioritizing paperwork over people work was the priority.

As a principal and director, I had an open door policy, and I encourage any educational leader who desires to be more effective to do the same. It is true that by having an open door policy, people might tend to poke their heads through your office door at the most inopportune times. However, I had an easy fix for this: I was never in my office unless an appointment was made. If people wanted to find me, they would find me in the hallways or classrooms interacting with my stakeholders.

When you finally get to sit in your office after the school day ends, you still have to remember that people come before paper. For example, you might be on the phone, running some numbers, reviewing some reports, or trying to chip away at an email inbox overflowing with messages, with all of the senders considering their message "urgent." Then, right in the middle of it all, stakeholders might poke their head into your door, see the look of intense focus on your face as your eyes are fixated on your computer screen, and ask, "Hey! Are you busy?" or "Hey! You got a minute or two?" When this happens, resist the temptation to roll your eyes and flash them a look that says, "Does it look like I'm busy?" Instead, smile as you remember that people come first. After all, when your office door is open, you are inviting others in, so when they actually do come in, you can't be mad about it.

I can remember spending late evenings in the office answering emails, signing checks, and writing up evaluations because during the school day, I would be on the bus ramp greeting students, at the car loop greeting parents, completing instructional rounds, doing café duty, monitoring the playground, and more. I did these things all in an effort to model for my school family that I was all in as their principal. One afternoon around three o'clock, after the buses had left, I was finally in my office and beginning my paperwork. A staff member came by wanting to discuss a personal matter. At first, she just stood there looking at me. I looked back at her and asked, "Is everything okay?" I could tell by the look on her face that it wasn't and that she needed some of my time. As I looked at the pile on my desk, I thought, *Oh my goodness, I have so much to do! You want to meet with me now?* However, I came from behind my desk and invited her to have a seat with me at the round table in my office. My round table is what I use to have conversations; to have serious discussions over a desk is more directive. I asked her if I needed to close the door, and she said yes. That's when I knew I would be there for a while – and I was. She was having some real personal issues that were impacting her performance. If she hadn't come to talk to me about them, she would have likely been written up for them at some point. However, the time we spent together that afternoon discussing her issue was priceless. Even though it cost me some precious time that I had scheduled for paperwork, it paid off in my being able to help one of my valuable staff assets get through a difficult time. That's People Before Paper.

Don't get me wrong. I know that there are going to be times when you just don't have the time to sit down and spend time with people, helping them work through issues, but there is a way to do it so that those whom you serve actually feel served, even when you put them off. For example, if I was standing in the school hallway in the morning during student drop-off and parents walked up to me and asked if they could talk to me, I would respond, "Sure! Is it something quick, or do you need some time?" If they said it was just a quick question, I would give them a few minutes right there on the spot. Even if I was busy, I would take the time to stop what I was doing, give them my undivided attention, look them in the eye, listen to what they were saying, empathize with what they were feeling, and then give them an answer. Yes, I knew that there were a lot of things going on around me that also needed my focus and attention, but I had to always remind myself that my primary reason for being there was to serve people, not push paper and drive processes and programs.

Here's another thing that I know: parents, or stakeholders in general, who have problems can be emotional, and being emotional can make them wordy – they want to explain every detail and every angle of the situation. If you tell them that you have a "quick minute" to answer a question, a wordy stakeholder might start talking and still will not have gotten to the main point or question five minutes later. As the leader, you have a lot to do, so being trapped in such a corner simply will not work. To prevent this, you'll have to master the art of giving them a couple of minutes to make their point, and if they don't get there, or if it seems like too much for you to address in a "Can I get a minute" interaction, you'll have to gently bring things to a close. My go-to approach was to give them a couple of minutes, and once I realized it was too big of an issue to handle on the spot, I would interject, saying, "Wow. I totally understand your issue. You're right to be concerned. You know, Mrs. Jones, I would like to give your concern some time and serious attention. Would you mind going into the office and making an appointment to come in to talk to me so we can really figure this thing out together? I really want to give this matter my full attention." Then, once I empathized with their feelings, validated their concerns, and redirected them, they would walk away satisfied they had been heard. I guess that's where I got the nickname "The parent whisperer!" From there, they would head to the office to make an appointment while I got back to the business of serving the other stakeholders.

It's not only your job to remember that people work comes before paperwork; it is also your job to ensure that you remind your team of leaders and administrators to embrace this principle. I have found that the best way to ensure that the People Before Paper principle permeates the environment and becomes a part of the culture is two-fold. First, you have to constantly reinforce to your team that you all are in the people business. No matter what, people come first. You should promote this principle at every staff or team meeting, at training, or review. Second, you simply need to model the principle in action. People Before Paper must become an integral part of your organization's fabric and exemplified by every leader at any level of leadership. However, it's one thing to be told to embrace a principle as a value of the organizational culture and it's another thing to have a living, breathing example that walks it out and shows everyone how it's done. That's your job, so use every opportunity you can to teach them what the principle practically looks like in action. When you do, you don't have to say, "See, everybody? I just exercised our People Before Paper principle. I just showed you how it's done." No, your people are smart. If you constantly reinforce the principle and model it before them without a word, they'll catch onto it. Have you heard the saying, "More is caught than is taught?" It's true in this case, too. Most people learn better by practical example and modeling than they do from training and lectures. Therefore, embrace the practice not only in word, but in action, and your team will follow suit.

I'm going to tell you something that a lot of educational leaders think but will rarely come out and say relating to People Before Paper: the people in your family deserve to be a priority, too. Did you know that one of the professional industries with the highest divorce rates is education, particularly among its leaders? The long hours, hard work, and mental and physical energy that educators invest into making their school successful can be all consuming. Your family can take a hit when you're an educational leader who is trying to be all things to all people in the schoolhouse, so you must be as intentional at prioritizing the people at home as you are about prioritizing the people on your job. I have experienced countless educators and colleagues over the years who have confided in me that the demands of their job were impacting their home lives. Of course, I gave them advice on how to strike a better balance between work and home, but for some, it was too late: they got divorced as did I. My advice to you is the same that I have given to others over the years, especially as I got older and more mature in my perspective of what really matters in life. If your job as an educational leader is impacting your family, I wholeheartedly recommend that you spend more time with your family. Take a mental health day. Go on that long weekend trip. Get someone to cover for you while you go to your children's games, recitals, and awards programs. Prioritize those people!

For the first part of my career, I had a 7 am to 7 pm rule. I worked 12 hours a day so I wouldn't have to take any work home with me. I realized that I had to give up some things in order to work these hours – like a social life during the week – but at least when I got home, I could give my full attention to my family. At first, I thought all of this was necessary. However, as I got deeper into the field, around year eight and my own divorce, I realized that I had to have boundaries. I had to find a way to get my work done without forsaking my son or my mental health.

I often had to remind myself and others that you get the same salary whether you work 12-hour days or 6-hour days. As long as you find a way to get the work done without sacrificing your and your family's well-being, you do whatever works for you. Learn the value of self-care, whatever that means for you, and care for your family in the midst of caring for those you lead at work. Otherwise, you'll surely get burned out along your leadership trajectory. The further along I went in my career, the more I learned the value of this principle. In fact, I began advising young people who were just beginning their careers in education to start prioritizing their families and themselves through self-care from the very beginning; don't wait until you begin to burn out and your family begins to fall apart to make such decisions. My advice: do everything you can for as many people as you can for as long as you can, but don't forget about yourself and your loved ones at home.

As an educational leader, you also need to be able to diagnose when people on your team might be having problems at home related to the amount of time, energy and resources they expend at work. If they are willing, talk to them about the problem and recommend that they give greater priority to their family at home. Then, be willing to provide whatever support you can to help them actually do this without leaving the tasks of the job undone. Toward the end of my career as a director of schools, I would put out a note to my principals that if they wanted me to run their school building while they got other things done, like observations, I would be more than happy to do so. For example, if they needed to get into the classrooms and do some observations, I would come in and stand in for them as they got this important work done. However, if they needed to tend to something with their families, attend a special family event, take a sick kid to the doctor, or even just take a day off to spend quality time with their loved ones, I would be there to stand in for them. This was gold! Not only did it increase my leadership influence and effectiveness with them, but it helped me to hold on to some really good people that I might otherwise have lost. The last thing you want is to lose good team members because they feel like they have to choose between their job and their family. When you prioritize the people on your team and support them so they can prioritize their families, everyone wins. Relationships matter!

③
HELP ME UNDERSTAND

Here's something that most building leaders won't tell you: they can't stand confrontation! They often spend a great deal of time thinking of ways to avoid confrontation at all costs. Some of them will even use passive aggressive means to confront the more aggressive stakeholders – particularly parents and teachers – they are responsible for leading. If you're the type of building leader who loathes confrontation and does whatever possible to avoid it, I'm here to help you with something that has worked so well for me over the years that if I could, I would shout it from the mountaintops!

I keep three words in my leadership toolbox that have revolutionized my leadership effectiveness for the past few decades: Help Me Understand. I learned these words and their power when I was in the principalship and as I transitioned to the role of director of schools. As a director, you have to have a lot of difficult, highly-sensitive dialogues that could "go left" if they are not handled correctly. The words "Help Me Understand" help to ensure the smooth facilitation of these interactions. I like to say that at the end of these dialogues, we might not agree, but at least we both understand. Help Me Understand takes difficult dialogues from being confrontational to being conversational.

When you understand the power of Help Me Understand, you'll never operate as a leader without them again. They are so effective that anybody can benefit from using them to confront issues. A director can use them with a principal, a principal can use them with a teacher, a teacher can even use them with a student (because teachers are leaders over the students in their classrooms). In fact, you can use these three little words with big impact in any area of life, from confronting issues in the home with family, with friends, in organizations you are a part of, or any other environment in which you are faced with confronting an issue. They are effective in any setting because they help you seek to understand rather than being understood.

As you are doing the work of an educational leader, or the work of any leader for that matter, you will often have to confront difficult issues without being confrontational. There's a difference between the two, and there's also a thin line. You must understand and recognize both, because if you are a building leader who approaches your team members the wrong way (i.e., you are overly confrontational), you could lose valuable team members, kill organizational morale, and alienate your followers. You could even become the target of subversion as your followers engage in passive-aggressive tactics designed to sabotage you. In other words, dealing with issues in a negative, confrontational way can decrease your leadership effectiveness.

QUEENISM

Stand and deliver! Sometimes, you have to stand up and say the tough things that people don't want to hear.

Nonetheless, as a leader, you can't be timid and effective at the same time; you must put your big boy or big girl pants on and deal with issues as they arise in order to be effective. Stand and deliver! Sometimes, you have to stand up and say the tough things that people don't want to hear. You can't run from them or turn a blind eye because you don't like confronting issues. If you do, the issues will only grow, spread to other team members, and become a cancer that poisons the entire organization. The only way to avoid this is to nip things in the bud, confronting issues without being confrontational. I've used Help Me Understand with gaining clarity on decisions that my staff members make dealing with everything from teacher assignments to discipline dispositions, and from handling difficult parents to problem-solving with students.

Regardless of the circumstance, these three words really work, giving you insight into how certain decisions were made. The best part is that using them as a non-confrontational confrontation tool keeps you from taking on an adversarial posture with your team member. Instead, you and the team member who made the questionable decision become two individuals on the same team who are working towards a better, more workable win for the organization. In the end, no one feels like the one who "lost," and there is no cause for resentment, because Help Me Understand introduces a sense of fairness into the interaction. Side note: Always try to avoid leaving your team members feeling resentful or bitter with you or your leadership, because this is not healthy for the culture of the school. Resentment might start with a disgruntled team member, but it will inevitably end up affecting your other stakeholders, like your students, parents and teachers, in some way.

There are going to be a lot of well-meaning people you lead who will make some thoughtless, problematic decisions that introduce a whole new set of problems that did not initially exist before the bad decision was made. When these decisions, or the brand new problems that have resulted from them, come to your attention, if you're like me, the first thing you'll do is shake your head and silently ask yourself, "What were they thinking when they made that decision?"

For example, when I heard that one of my teachers had said to a kid, "Shut up! And you can go home and tell your mother that I said it!" Of course, the first words that came to my mind were, *What was she thinking?* I needed her to Help Me Understand. In another instance, I had to deal with a situation in which the principal made a problematic decision without thinking things all the way through. This principal was a new principal at the school. In his zeal, as soon as he arrived at the school, he met with the teachers to find out what they didn't like and what they wanted to see changed in the school. He wanted to gain immediate favor with the teachers and make them happy because the last principal had not done so. The teachers convinced the principal to change the way the students were dropped off at the building; they wanted a "one stop shop" drop-off process, which would make things easier and more convenient for them in the mornings. To appease the teachers, the principal simply went ahead and made the change; he did not consult with the parents (or anyone else for that matter) about how this change would impact the other stakeholders. Needless to say, unbelievable bottlenecks occurred as soon as the new drop-off process went into effect. It was *crazy* outside of the school building! Horns were blowing, parents were late for work and fussing, and there was utter chaos.

Of course, as the school director, I heard about this situation. I went to the school and said to him, "Where did this decision to change things come from? Help me understand." He explained the process of arriving at the decision: he met with the teachers, the teachers wanted it, and he wanted to get into their good graces and fix what they didn't like about their old principal in order to get a quick win with them, so he gave them what they wanted. Once I understood his thought process, I first explained to him that his initial mistake was one that many new principals make: meeting with the teachers and asking them what changes they wanted. His second mistake was focusing on making the teachers happy; their happiness is important, but it is not the school's priority. A building leader should keep teachers happy up to the point that it begins to affect the happiness of the other stakeholders, primarily the children. After that, I explained that changes in the school could include the desires of the staff, but the decisions should ultimately be made based on the principal's own observations and his consideration of how the decision will impact every stakeholder in the school. Everyone other than the teachers was blindsided by the new drop-off process, and this should never be the case with such a significant decision.

Finally, I explained that it wasn't the changing of the drop-off process that was the mistake; it was how the decision was made. There is a proper way to make decisions in a school – thinking things all the way through and involving all who will be affected – particularly decisions that impact everyone in the school.

My advice to him was the kind of support that a school director should offer to building leaders. Then, I asked him, based on what I had just shared with him, to rethink the same situation. "What will you do differently in the future, and why? Walk me through this. Help me understand your thought process." When all was said and done, he realized that when he was considering making a decision that impacted everyone, he needed to talk to the people the decision would impact before making it. In the same situation, he should have talked to the parents, the PTA board, and anyone else who would be affected. He should have done a run-through before deciding that this was the new drop-off process to see how it would work. While he talked things through with me, I could see the A-ha moment he was having. He had never thought of things this way before, and he appreciated the time I took with him to arrive at this discovery. In asking him to Help Me Understand, I had also helped him understand and arrive at a better way of making decisions for his school in the future.

If this hasn't happened to you as a leader yet, just hang in there; your day is coming. You're going to hear about decisions your followers made that will leave you racking your brain trying to figure out how any educator could make such a decision. It doesn't make logical sense, intellectual sense, or even common sense; it's impossible to make meaning out of bad decisions. Let me save you some time. Before you sit there trying to figure out what your follower was thinking (because it's literally impossible to "figure out" things that make no sense), and before you start to fuss or to try to get your point across, simply say the following three simple words: Help Me Understand.

Help Me Understand signals to your team member that you are trying to understand the rationale and thought process they used when making the decision to say or do what they did. Believe it or not, when you say, "Help me understand," many times, this will be the *very first* time that the individual who made the decision took the time to think through the decision! Here's something I've learned as a leader over the years: people make decisions all the time without critically thinking through them. They often take a surface-level assessment of an issue before they make a decision and then they take action. This means that they don't consider the issue from all stakeholder perspectives and they don't evaluate how their decision is going to impact everyone involved.

On more than one occasion I have also had to use Help Me Understand when trying to get to the root of a problem between stakeholders. For example, a parent would call the principal's office and complain about something a teacher did to their child. I would ask the parent to Help Me Understand why they were upset and what they wanted. After I understood the parent's perspective, the wrong thing to do as a leader would be to listen to everything the parent said and take their words at face value. In order to truly operate out of Help Me Understand, I had to confront the teacher with the parent's complaint and ask the teacher to Help Me Understand his or her perspective. Then, after I understood both sides of the situation, I could make a decision, considering everyone who would be impacted by it – the parent, teacher and student – and find a way for everyone to meet on middle ground.

In order to maximize the effectiveness of Help Me Understand as a confrontational tool, you have to get the timing right. As soon as you see that one of your team members made a bad decision that created a different set of problems that did not previously exist, pull Help Me Understand out of your toolbox. Don't sit on the words; pull them out immediately. Then, allow them to respond.

The way that people usually respond to your Help Me Understand invitation tends to fall into three categories:

- **"The Confessor"** – Sometimes, you can say, "Help me understand" to someone who made a bad decision, and they will just openly confess, "I don't know what I was thinking. I wasn't thinking at all. I'm sorry." They know that they have no argument or defense for the decision they made, so they don't even waste their breath trying. I can respect this, because it allows us to get to a point of, "Let's do better in the future by really thinking through things before taking action, and let me know what I can do to support you!" faster.

- **"The Epiphany-getter"** – This is the bad decision maker who sets out with the purpose of explaining a decision, searching their mind for a way to help you understand that their decision was a good one. However, as they begin thinking deeply, comprehensively and critically and talking through their decision, a lightbulb will come on; they have an epiphany. You can often see this moment of "Ah-ha!" on their face as they lead into the realization that their decision wasn't a sound, well thought-out one after all. This is usually followed by an apology like, "I can see where I went wrong now. I get it. I apologize, and it won't happen again." Again, I can appreciate this level of honesty and transparency. It shows me that the individual was not trying to "win the confrontation" but was open enough to see and admit where they went wrong. This opens the door for me to come in and say, "Great! I'm glad you see that. In the future, if you need to run an idea by me before taking action, I'm here for you!"

- **"The Defender"** – While some people will hear your Help Me Understand as an open and fair invitation to share their "side of the story," others will see it as a challenge or a threat. These individuals will take on a defensive posture when explaining their decisions and actions. Because there is literally no way to make sense out of something nonsensical, they will not be able to give you a clear, comprehensible rationale for their actions. However – and here's the problem – they will often see but will never admit that they were wrong. When you ask them additional questions to help them see that what they are saying is not making sense, they will only grow agitated and frustrated, complaining about how you are questioning and challenging them. The reality is that they know that they were wrong and cannot explain their way out of their decision. Ultimately, because they are unwilling to cooperate with the process, all you can do is let them know that when they make such decisions, you cannot support them. Then, you'll have to apologize to all who were affected by the decision on behalf of the school's leadership.

Side note: Unlike the Defender, the Confessor and the Epiphany-getter reach the point where they say, "I apologize." These are two of the most powerful, important words that any educational leader can say.

Let me warn you that your initial response to hearing that someone on your team made what you consider to be an absurd or senseless decision will be to go to the person and say, "You shouldn't have done that! You obviously didn't think things through. What you decided was a bad decision. What I would have done was..." and then you go on to tell the person all the reasons the decision was a bad one and what they should have done instead. You do all the talking (which is, in reality, scolding, and which never turns out well) and they do all the listening.

The problem with this is that when you do all of the talking, you are the one using your logic and intellect to process every part of the decision from start to finish. Good for you. However, where's the learning experience in this for your team member who made the decision? Sure, you're their leader, so they have no choice but to sit there and listen to you tell them how wrong they are, but I guarantee they will be sitting there thinking that they were right and that your stance is wrong. After they endure your rebuke, they will walk away unchanged, liable to use the same logic (or lack thereof) when approaching future decision making moments. Another reason to avoid telling them what to do is that they can always come back and say that you told them to do this or that. If they do what you directed them to do instead of what they realized on their own what they should do, if what you told them to do ends up producing an undesirable outcome in the future, they will always point their fingers toward you and say, "This is your fault. I only do what you told me to do, so I'm not to blame." To avoid this, allow them to arrive at the decision and own it, because then they are personally responsible for it.

When wielding this powerful confrontational tool, always keep in mind that Help Me Understand isn't really for you; it's designed to be a learning and growth opportunity for the person who made the bad decision. I know that there will be some building leaders who say, "I'm not about to do all of that, Dr. McQueen! I already understand why they did what they did. They weren't thinking, so they made a bonehead decision! Forget not being confrontational. I'm going to just tell them that they were dead wrong. Sometimes, you've got to take authority and let people know who's boss!" Of course, since you're the boss, you can do things in whatever way you feel. However, just know that anytime you "boss up" against your teammates, you create a context in which you and your ego win and they lose – and most people don't handle losing well. When you approach your team member or leader this way, the interaction is not going to end well, and you're eventually going to have some organizational culture problems on your hands.

What your objective should be in situations like these should be two-fold. First, it should be to help those who make less-than-ideal decisions to arrive at the conclusion that their decision was an ill-advised one all on their own. There is little to no benefit in your telling them why their decision was not a good one, but there is *great* benefit in allowing them to arrive at the conclusion that their decision was not a good one themselves. In other words, there is value in discovery versus direction. Discovery allows them to arrive at and own their own decision. Whatever people discover on their own, they are more likely to retain. They won't make the same mistake again because they have taken the time to think through why their way was not the best approach. Direction, however, takes the power out of their ability to arrive at and change their belief of how they were wrong because you, the leader, are simply telling them – directing them – on what they should have done.

The best way to lead people to discovery is to simply say, "Help me understand." In speaking these words, you are inviting that person to enter a critical thinking moment, giving you the backstory and rationale behind whatever decision was made. The power of a critical thinking moment is that the conclusions it yields have a lasting impact on the individual, influencing his or her decisions in the future. This reduces the likelihood that they will ever use the same logic pathway to process and make the same ill-advised decision again.

Your second objective with using Help Me Understand should be to open the dialogue for the support your leaders need if they are not clear on the "why" behind their decision making. Help Me Understand is a tool that tasks an individual with turning a decision in and out and upside in order to make sense of it so that the rationale is not only clear to them but to the recipient of their explanation. This is easier said than done, especially since it's often being done for the first time by the person who made the decision. However, even though it can be difficult, it is an indispensable exercise that leaders should not skip. Why? Because taking people through it reinforces that whenever an organizational decision is made, one must always consider how the decision will impact everyone in the organization, not just a few. If you are a building leader, you already know that your perspective must be one that takes every stakeholder's vision into account. However, you cannot take for granted that everyone to whom you have entrusted decision-making power operates based on the same perspective.

For example, let's say you're a principal, and a parent calls you with a problem. From a building leader perspective, it seems like an easy problem to fix; all you'd need to do is make one decision, the parent's problem would go away, and you would be the hero. However, you must be careful of making knee-jerk decisions to fix problems when they arrive. This means, before you make the "easy" decision that will immediately address someone's issue, problem or concern, consider how your solution will not just impact that person but everyone else in the building. Most people do not think this broadly when making a decision to fix a problem. They think of how to bring immediate relief to whoever is being inconvenienced by the problem so they can check it off their list and move on to addressing the next problem. However, after you have challenged them with enough Help Me Understand exercises, they become much more deliberative and calculated in the decisions they make. Rather than make them flippantly or without critical thought, they invest more consideration into them. This lasting effect that Help Me Understand can have on your followers can have a priceless impact on the way the leaders in your organization operate!

4

TRUST AND VERIFY

Let me share something with you that I have always shared with building leaders under my mentorship: all roads lead back to the principal's office. Another way of saying this is that all fingers point back to the leader. Most leaders will agree with this principle in theory; however, in practice, they often come up with reasons to disagree with it. When you say you understand that all roads lead back to the principal's office and you're the principal or the building leader, you are saying that no matter what happens in that building, it's your responsibility. If a teacher says the wrong thing the wrong way to a parent, it's the principal's responsibility. If the students don't hit their testing benchmarks because the teachers were ineffective in preparing them, it's the principal's responsibility. When the test scores come out, they don't put each teacher's name on the scores of the students they taught; they put the school name and the principal's name on those documents. If student athletes are not making the grade but are still allowed to play, it's the principal's responsibility.

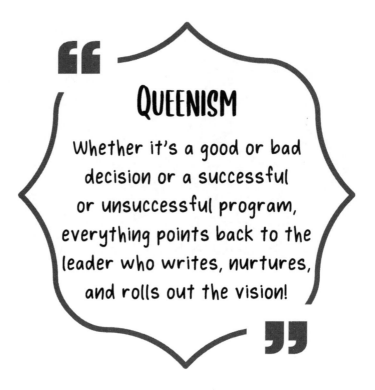

QUEENISM

Whether it's a good or bad decision or a successful or unsuccessful program, everything points back to the leader who writes, nurtures, and rolls out the vision!

Everything that happens on that campus is ultimately the principal's responsibility because all roads lead back to the principal's office. Some kind of way, the principal is always the one who has to answer for all of the stakeholders' experiences at the school. Whether it's a good or bad decision or a successful or unsuccessful program, everything points back to the leader who writes, nurtures, and rolls out the vision!

I say that leaders almost always agree with this principle in theory but end up singing a different song when it comes to practice. At the most fundamental level, they agree that they are the leader of the school, so whatever happens under the roof of the building they lead is within their authority to change. However, I say that they end up singing a different song when it comes to the practice of the principle, because when someone tries to hold them accountable for something that happened in the building, they blame someone else. That teacher teaches poorly. The department leader didn't budget properly. The student doesn't try hard enough. The parents aren't doing their part in the home. These leaders try to find someone else to take the blame, but the reality is that, as the building leader, it all falls on them.

I understand that it's challenging to be responsible for a building where there are lots of people with different levels of responsibility and accountability, and everything they do reflects back on you as the building leader. That can make a leader feel quite a bit of pressure. People ask, "How can I practically be responsible for ensuring that the 100 people in this building are doing the right things at the right times? What can I do to ensure that their slip-ups don't end up reflecting negatively on me, especially when I can't keep my finger on what they are doing day to day?" I have an answer for you. It's called "Trust and Verify."

Trust and Verify is a process of ensuring that what should get done in the building gets done according to your vision. It basically consists of you making assignments and delegating tasks and having the confidence in the people that you gave them to, believing that they will get them done. After all, you wouldn't have assigned them the task or assignment if you did not feel that they could complete it. The sole fact that you delegated the assignments is an indication of your trust in your team members; you have no doubt that the job will be completed, according to your specifications. You can sleep soundly at night knowing that you gave some important tasks to some very capable people, whom you trust. The only thing left to do to close the loop is to verify that the task or assignment is on pace to get done, and at the deadline, that it actually got done. Engaging Trust and Verify in your leadership process saves you from misunderstandings, miscommunications, disappointments, unwelcomed surprises, and the detrimental outcomes that can potentially result from them.

You might be saying, "Dr. McQueen, if I trust people, why do I need to verify that things got done? Doesn't that suggest that I don't trust my people?" The answer is "No." Verifying that the work you assigned is getting done doesn't suggest a lack of trust; it suggests that you understand that all roads lead back to the principal's office! When you verify the completion of assigned tasks, the intent is not to communicate "I don't think you're doing / you did the work." Instead, the intent of verifying is to communicate, "Let me review your progress / your finished work so I can check its completion off in my principal's register. I will be held personally responsible for it, so it's important for me to be able to report on something that I'm accountable for, right?" When you clarify this understanding with the people you lead, you will come across less like an overlord and more like the responsible leader that you are.

Someone asked me if trusting and verifying was something that I just did or if it was something that I actually told my team that I was doing as their leader. I find a great deal of value in actually saying the words to my team members, especially my newer ones, because it helps me to establish my expectations of them from the very beginning of our work relationship. Stating the principle and explaining it is especially important when bringing on team members who are new leaders in their respective roles. You can't hold them accountable to a principle without helping them to understand it first. Letting your team members know that you will Trust and Verify is less a warning to them than it is a warning for them. Not only is it something that you will do to ensure that the things for which you will be held personally responsible as the principal are accomplished the way you want them done, but it is something that you want for your staff to soak in and start doing themselves as they assign and delegate tasks to others.

Trusting and verifying is important for you to implement if you will increase your effectiveness as an educational leader. A lot of times, the principal or leader will trust that a teacher has made the call back to a parent, sent a form in, or successfully completed whatever was assigned to them. However, I can tell you from decades of experience that trust alone is not enough. You can't just walk in optimism and rely on good faith in your workers to give you the peace and confidence that they got things done; you have to verify that they were completed. I have never met a leader who said they regretted using Trust and Verify. Instead, they have consistently expressed that as unpopular as the practice might be, they are glad they trusted and even more glad that they verified. It has saved many a leader from being blindsided by incomplete projects, tasks and assignments for which the leader him or herself would have to ultimately answer. Remember: all roads lead back to the principal's office.

It is possible that you may be thinking that Trust and Verify sounds like micromanagement, and people don't like to be micromanaged. However, micromanagement is about checking in along every part of the process, while verifying is more about checking in before the final deliverables are due to be presented. I see verifying more as a necessary part of a collaborative effort to achieve the same goal in an educational setting. To accomplish this, I cast the vision for what needs to be done, my people do their part and notify me once certain milestones are achieved, and I build in checkpoints along the way to examine what they've done, making sure things were done according to how they were laid out in the vision. This is important, because sometimes people will get things done, but the quality of what they did is lacking because it reflects their subjective preferences and standards rather than the vision. Therefore, when you Trust and Verify, you're not just checking to see that things are done, but you are checking to see if they are done in the spirit of the vision in mind.

Here's an example that shows the importance of Trust and Verify. When I was a principal, we used what was called the Child Study Process. When students were having difficulty, they would go before a panel of people to discuss the difficulty that they were having. Sometimes, parents would request an evaluation of the student to see if their child had some sort of learning deficiency. When parents requested these evaluations, I trusted my team to ensure that the evaluation was done. On one occasion, on a date after the evaluation was supposed to be done, we showed up at the big committee meeting to discuss the student's progress and review the evaluation results, only to find out that the evaluation had not been completed. This was a surprise to me, but it should not have been; if I had trusted and verified before the meeting that the testing had occurred, this situation would never have happened. The staff member who was responsible for getting the evaluation completed stepped up and apologized, admitting that she was in error. She said she had missed it and that the date had gotten away from her. I respected her for doing this because that's what leaders do; they take responsibility for their actions. I apologized to the parent, who was also at the meeting, for my staff missing this critical piece of the study. So much of our understanding of the child's needs was to come from that evaluation, and it was inexcusable that we hadn't performed it.

Afterwards, as I was debriefing with my staff about the meeting and our failure, a member on the committee became very defensive and went to bat for the staff member who had already admitted her wrong. She said to me, "Well, the parent was being very ugly and rude in the way that she was talking to us at the Child Study meeting. She didn't have to talk to us like that. It was uncalled for." I couldn't give her a pass on this. So as not to embarrass her in the meeting, I told her that we would talk after the meeting. I wanted to keep this confrontation private.

Once we were alone in my office, I said, "Wait a minute! Help me understand why you are making excuses for something that was clearly missed." There was no explanation she could offer. I said, "I don't care how the parent acted or what she said; this dropped ball was not the parent's fault. It was ours. This cannot happen again!" The counselor was upset at being confronted, and she cried. However, it had to be done. The moral of the story is simply Trust and Verify. If I had trusted and verified rather than trusting and taking for granted that things were going to get done, none of this would have had to happen. There would have been no excuses for bad behavior and no need for defensiveness, which can totally derail the productivity of a meeting. When you trust but do not verify, you open yourself up to being blindsided, embarrassed, or placed in the uncomfortable position of having to confront people over tasks that are unfinished or that lack the quality necessary to realize the intended vision.

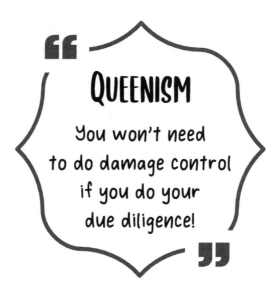

QUEENISM

You won't need to do damage control if you do your due diligence!

On another occasion with less-critical implications, I was working with a committee chair to put together an awards assembly. I delegated the ordering of all materials needed for the assembly to her and trusted that she would take care of it. However, when I went to verify that the materials had been ordered, I discovered that they had not ordered what was needed for every award category. The job was being done, but it was not being done completely – according to the vision. Needless to say, she was embarrassed. However, we were able to print certificates for the categories she missed and have them ready for distribution at the awards ceremony the next day. That's another thing with Trust and Verify: when you verify and discover that things are not done, you'll need to overcome the obstacle by thinking on your feet. Always have a plan B in your pocket, just in case. However, you won't need to do damage control if you do your due diligence.

Trust and Verify can be used at various levels of task assignment. For example, when I was a principal, I would be sitting around the table with my team, and my team members would give me some data. I trusted the data was correct, but I couldn't just trust the integrity of the data at face value; I needed to verify its accuracy. Thus, I would ask my team members to go through the data and explain to me how it was collected and their understanding of what it meant. If they did an adequate job in their explanation, my trust was affirmed, and I was ready to take responsibility for the data.

Most leaders know that managing people can be tricky. People are already sensitive and suspicious enough as it is. When you add Trust and Verify to the formula, for some people, this might feel like a problem. They don't like feeling like someone is going to follow up on the tasks and assignments they were given to complete. When people are outspoken and resistant to the notion of their leader following up on them, the question I want to ask them is "What are you afraid of?" People who don't like their leaders to follow up on them usually feel this way because of fear; if they don't want to do the work or are not sure that they are going to see it through to completion, they don't want to be called to the carpet on it. They want to do poor work without anyone saying anything about it. They want to be comfortable while doing things with a spirit of mediocrity. Unfortunately, a leader cannot run a school effectively this way, especially since the consequences for the person's poor work are going to pave a road that leads right back to the principal's office. If a team member or leader wants to do less-than-excellent work, they should not be allowed to do it in peace at your school. You, the building leader, have to confront anyone who does not do the work you assign in accordance with the vision you outlined.

When I was a director of schools, I had some principals who told me that there were some issues that they had attempted to verify, only to discover that the individual they had trusted with a task came up lacking. However, they also said that they didn't confront the individual because they didn't want to have a drag on their climate or to have negativity permeate the building. They thought that not confronting trust violations would maintain the peace in the school and keep the atmosphere light and happy. These principals wanted to be liked. I had to explain to them that by not confronting trust violations, they were doing more harm to their school environment than good. They avoided the confrontations because they wanted "everyone to be happy," when in reality, if the individual who did not perform up to par is happy, you can bet that there are others who will not be happy – like the students and parents.

Typically, the people that the building leader is scared to confront impact the entire building. These scary-to-confront individuals are usually strong, aggressive, domineering teachers, which I call "toxic teachers." The toxic teacher is a drag on the school's climate; a negative cloud looming over what should be a positive atmosphere. Their below-par performance and steadfast defense of who they are and how they work typically earns them a reputation of being hard to deal with and disliked by most of the school. There's no getting around it; they must be confronted or else they and their effect on your school environment will always be there. I've had to deal with many toxic teachers over the years. I was never afraid or intimidated to confront them because I always did it in a way that ensured I maintained my dignity and ensured that they maintained theirs. In other words, I did it in such a way that we addressed the problem while both saving face.

If you do not confront stakeholders that compromise the quality standards of the educational environment by their behavior, by poor work, or by not representing the values of the organization, it's going to swing around back to you. Someone will end up confronting you about it. For example, if you have a teacher who is yelling at students or not meeting her professional responsibilities and you, the building leader, do not follow up on the situation, it's only a matter of time before a parent calls you. Even worse, you might get a call from central administration, because the parent has escalated the matter up the ranks. When central administration calls you, they will have one question for you: "Why didn't you confront that issue?" It's not enough for you to set your team and leaders loose, trusting them to represent the school in the best way possible; you have to verify that they are doing so, and you have to immediately confront situations when your verification shows that your trust has been violated.

QUEENISM

Leadership is the invisible rope that pulls other people to greatness. They don't even know they are being pulled!

When you Trust and Verify and then confront staff members when your verification shows that things are not being done according to your vision, it's not personal; it's problem solving. It has nothing to do with you, the leader, or the team member who received the assignment. It's about making sure that together, we meet the needs and address the problems of the school so that the children can get the best quality education possible. Will these confrontations always go smoothly? No. There will inevitably be times when you get a negative reaction from the people you are trying to hold accountable for executing tasks according to your vision. However, negative reactions come along with the leadership territory, so you might as well get used to it. It's human nature for people to push back when you challenge them for not doing the best job they can possibly do. As you are trying to help them rise to their next level of professionalism and performance, some people will resist simply because they have been programmed to think that average is okay. However, don't let their resistance deter you, and don't be afraid to lead. Leadership is the invisible rope that pulls other people to greatness. They don't even know they are being pulled! As long as you are leading from the heart, people may not like being followed up on, but they will respect your work as a building leader because although they may not admit it, they know you're simply taking care of business.

⑤ TEACHERS HAVE JOBS

I love teachers, and I love kids more. Because of this, it is my firm position that everything we do as educators should be all about the kids. Absolutely nothing comes before the kids we are responsible for educating and preparing for a successful future. This is a necessary conversation to have with educators because a lot of times, educators, from the principal on down, can let their personal preferences or their desire for things to be the most comfortable and convenient for them get in the way of what is best for the students.

QUEENISM

I love teachers, and I love kids more!

I have a great deal of gratitude for teachers and the skills they possess. They are the hardest working folks in the building (outside of the custodians, if you have a good custodial staff – they are the lifeblood of the school). Let me tell you something: it is *hard* to replace a good teacher. In fact, it is easier to replace a principal than a good teacher, especially what I call a "total package teacher." This is the kind of teacher who can teach, is fun and likeable, can build relationships with the students, is an asset to the team, and goes above and beyond the duties listed on the job description to contribute to the success of the school community. When I had good teachers, I did all I could to hold on to them. This is mostly because I believe that you have to make sure you have happy teachers in order to have happy kids.

That said, I must also tell you that there is a limit that I'm willing to put on teachers' happiness: I will cater to teachers' happiness up to the point that their happiness stands to disrupt the happiness of the kids. Kids' happiness is essential to their being able to learn and getting them graduated with a quality education is the ultimate goal. This brings me to the point of my next principle: Teachers Have Jobs.

As both a principal and a director of schools, I would tell my leaders all the time, "At the end of the day, you already have a job. Your priority needs to be setting aside your own interests and doing everything it takes to help these kids get a job in the future." The Teachers Have Jobs principle is simply about ensuring that you keep the interests of the kids primary, even when it costs the teachers and school staff some convenience and comfort. This doesn't mean that you treat your teachers like their interests and desires don't matter; they should be reminded that they matter *a lot*. However, what matters more is what is in the best interest of the kids.

Just by introducing this concept, I know I might be ruffling some feathers. Leaders are sensitive about their teachers and keeping them happy, as they should be. Remember, I have already explained that I have a great deal of appreciation and respect for teachers, especially the "total package teachers." I'm well aware of how building leaders think about their teachers. They think, "Yeah, I understand doing what's best for the students, but if I lose this teacher, I don't know that I can find another teacher as good as this one. I don't want to lose my teachers by not putting their interests first!" This is especially a big consideration in a hard-to-staff building where the leader is hungry for warm bodies. It's already hard enough trying to get people to come work at the school, so they don't want to rock the boat with their teachers by not prioritizing the teachers' happiness.

I'm a witness to the fact that you can have happy teachers and happy students – and by happy students, I mean students whose interests are primary in the school, over and above all others. If your teachers are good teachers who work from the heart, knowing that the students are happy will make them happy as well. The teachers have degrees and jobs, and if they left their current jobs, they could go and get another job. Their role as educational leaders is to ensure that the kids can get jobs and start businesses, and in so doing, sustain our communities. Teachers should gain a great deal of satisfaction and joy from knowing that when they put the kids' interests first, they are equipping the next generation of community leaders and citizenry who will take the lead on shaping the society in which the teachers will also live. Thus, the investments they make into their kids by keeping the kids' interests first not only benefits the kids but the teachers and the world in which they will all live together.

When I worked as a director with oversight of several schools in the district, I would often find administrators making policy changes in their building based solely on the teachers' perspectives. They made shifts and changes in how things were done in order to make the teachers happy without giving critical thought to how these same changes were going to impact the students. For example, in one elementary school, the teachers asked the administration if they could change the school policy for third graders so that instead of teaching multiple subjects to their one homeroom class throughout the day, they would only have to teach one subject to different classes of students throughout the day. I immediately understood why they'd made such a request: it was easier and more comfortable for them. Instead of having to prepare lessons on reading, math, social studies, art, and other instructional topics, all they had to prepare for was one subject area. They wanted only to be accountable for teaching the one subject that they had studied in college, or that they simply preferred to teach. Mind you, this required students to collect their things and go from class to class throughout the day, each classroom representing a different subject area. When I found out about this change, I asked the question, "Did anyone think about the students before making this change?" The teachers asked for the change for their own comfort and convenience, but what about the students' comfort and convenience? Wouldn't it be better for students of such an early school age to stay in the same classroom with the same teacher throughout the day because of the relational bond they would develop that would facilitate learning? Wouldn't staying in the same classroom or homeroom throughout the school day bring them a greater sense of comfort and security? Then, consider how much disruption could potentially occur as the students gathered their things and walked from class to class!

Ultimately, I had to remind the administrators that any decisions they made had to include the comfort, convenience, interests and well-being of students first and foremost, even at the expense of the teachers. When those same teachers were in school, their teachers sacrificed these things for them so they could receive a high-quality education in a comfortable environment that would prepare them to get a good job and have a successful future. Now that they were grown and had jobs, it was time for them to pay it forward for the students they taught. Teachers already have jobs (although they don't get paid nearly enough for the jobs they do). Sometimes, they must sacrifice their comfort and convenience so the students they teach can have jobs one day, too.

QUEENISM

We don't teach content; we teach children!

I remember one story that happened when I was an elementary school principal. Based on the Teachers Have Jobs principle, I was determined to make staffing decisions based on student need versus teacher preference. I would have all of the teachers complete preference forms each year to share with me which grade they would like to teach; very rarely would they request to change grades. I usually met with each teacher to share where they would be the next year if they did not get their preferred grade. This particular year, I met with a 2nd grade teacher and shared with her that she would be moving to the 5th grade. She was an aspiring leader and had not taught a grade level for which standardized testing was performed. I said to her, "You need to be on a grade where there's standardized testing so that when you go to interview for leadership positions, you can say you taught that grade and can do standardized teaching." In light of her aspirations to become a leader, and in light of the academic, social and emotional needs of my 5th grade students, I thought it would be a great move. I always say, "We don't teach content; we teach children." In other words, we don't just teach the subject area; we teach kids how to sit up straight, pay attention, etc. – anything needed for "whole child" teaching. Considering this teacher's skills, I thought she would be a good fit for the move to 5th grade.

However, when I told her about the move, she began to cry! She said that she did not want to move; she wanted to continue teaching 2nd grade. I reminded her that her certification was K-5, so she would be fine teaching 5th grade. Still, her protest stood; she wasn't budging. Then, I learned what her biggest issue was. "How dare you break up our team!" she cried. Apparently, she had gotten used to working with and had bonded with the other 2nd grade teachers, so she was intent on staying with the 2nd grade, despite my needing her skills for the 5th grade students. I reminded her that we worked for the children and did what was best for them, not what was most comfortable and convenient for the teachers. The conversation ended with me telling her that I could just move her, but I wasn't going to do that. I hoped she would want to go to the 5th grade, but I would not force her to move. She was satisfied with that. She felt she'd gotten her way. Then, she went to the toxic teacher space: the break room. She told the other teachers all about how she'd stood up to me, held her position and gotten her way. Of course, it got back to me; what happens in the break room *never* stays in the break room; I used to tell my people to stay out of the break room, because it's such a toxic environment. Since my primary interest was still to ensure that the students' needs were met, so do you know what I did? I moved all of the other 2nd grade teachers to other grades and left the protesting teacher right where she was – in the 2nd grade. Teachers already have jobs. They are responsible for doing what is best for the kids so the kids can get jobs, too!

Years later, this same teacher became an assistant principal and was put in the same predicament. She told her building principal, "Now, I understand! This is not about the teachers and what they want. It's about the children and what *they* need!" I was pleased to see that she finally understood the principle that Teachers Have Jobs.

QUEENISM

Don't hire fast.
Hire well!

One of the times when the Teachers Have Jobs conversation is most pertinent is during the hiring process. It should be intuitive among educators that every hiring decision should be student-centered, based on which candidates will serve the students in the school best. However, you might be surprised to discover how often this is not the primary hiring criteria. For example, I've been in situations where I had a team of teachers who participated in interviewing and selecting candidates for an open teaching position at the school. I would have a "cracker jack" candidate whose training, credentials and experience were top of the line and who would be an exceptional choice to serve our students well. However, while the teachers on the hiring team thought the candidate was exceptional on paper, they didn't like the way he or she vibed with their group personality-wise. Since they didn't think the person would blend into their group well, they wanted to reject the candidate! I would hear such discussions and be appalled. I would remind them, "You already have a job. This hiring decision is not about what's best for you; it's about what's best for the students. You're not a reading specialist and this candidate is an exceptional one, so we're hiring her. She's going to help our kids get to where you are in life: employed with a good job!" Then, I would make the decision to hire the candidate. I didn't hire her because I was out of time and needed to fill a slot on my teaching staff; I hired her because of the quality of what she had to offer to our students. I never felt the pressure to hire fast; I always felt the responsibility to hire well.

6

LEAD AND LIFT

When most people think of leading, they think of moving forward and bringing all of their followers along with them. However, the most effective leaders do not simply move people forward; they lift them up as they go. I refer to this principle as "Lead and Lift."

The essence of Lead and Lift is that as you, the building leader, lift, inspire, and motivate your followers, you elevate your level of influence with them. This increased level of influence gives you the power to get your followers to execute and perform for you when you need them to. I know from first-hand experience that Lead and Lift is one of the most instrumental ways to increase your leadership effectiveness as an educational leader. There is an art and a science to leadership, which are embodied in Lead and Lift.

QUEENISM

There is an art
and a science
to leadership.

Lead and Lift is an investment that consists of making your staff members better versions of themselves for the benefit of the organization. It also includes making them feel good about their work and how it contributes to the organization's ability to accomplish its mission. When you inspire, lift, and motivate people, helping them to see that they are significant to the team and the lifeblood of the organization, the return on this investment is loyalty. You know that you've employed Lead and Lift effectively as a leader when you can ask your team of leaders to do tough things, and they gladly accept these assignments with a smile. They'll be willing to do anything for you, because they will feel that you've done so much for them!

One thing that I have noticed throughout my educational career is that a lot of leaders tend to primarily focus on leading – they drive people to things to get done based on obedience and requirements – while others tend to primarily focus on lifting – they keep people feeling good about the work they are doing whether they are meeting their goals or not. If you are going to be an effective leader, you cannot do one or the other; you have to do both. You have to Lead *and* Lift. It's like a see-saw. If you put too much weight on one end, the other end falls to the ground. If you spend all of your time leading and never lifting, all of your folks will fall to the ground. If you spend all of your time lifting and not leading, your work will fall to the ground. It does a school no good when the people are feeling good but the work outcomes are bad. For example, if there is a warm, positive, caring culture in the school but the fifth-grade kids are reading at a third-grade level because the work isn't getting done, that's no good. This is why it is essential that you learn to both Lead *and* Lift. When you learn to effectively balance leading with lifting, you will push the people to get the essential work done, but in the process, the people will feel that you care about them. You cannot do one without the other and be an effective leader. Leading and lifting is a beautiful dance, when it's done right.

I have found that the best way to Lead and Lift your team of leaders is through inspirational vision, professional development, motivation, and acknowledgement and appreciation.

First, inspirational vision helps to lift people as you lead them. Everything we do as leaders should begin with casting an inspirational vision. Why? Because an inspiring vision motivates and encourages people to want to give their all and do their best. It's true that you can lead people to do things without lifting them, but any success you achieve will be shallow and short-lived. The people you lead won't be invested and committed to the cause; they'll just half-heartedly do what you tell them to do because you're the boss and they know they need to obey you in order to keep their job. There's no win-win in that. As a leader, you should always be seeking wins all around. Win-wins for the administrator and the principal, for the principal and the teachers, and most of all, wins for everyone and the students. Getting things done through leadership in such a way that everyone wins and feels good about it is important for the organization.

This includes leading while lifting, inspiring and motivating the people you lead to get things done in a way that is consistent with the vision you promote.

Next, professional development helps to lift the people you lead. This kind of lifting doesn't have to be formal, like a professional seminar with a PowerPoint presentation and handouts. Professional development can be as simple as pulling one of your team members aside and giving them some coaching when you see something. Remember, as a leader, it's your responsibility to say something when you see something that's not quite right happening in your organization. This should be a part of your organization's culture that everyone in the building embraces. If you see something, say something! When you see your cafeteria worker speaking to students the wrong way, you can't just ignore it; you need to pull the worker aside when the lunch rush is over and offer some advice on how to handle the students in a more professional way. Not only does it count as professional development, but it lifts the worker by helping them to become better. By the way, don't limit lifting through professional development to your teachers and office workers. Everyone else, from the custodians to the cafeteria workers and the ground crew can be lifted in order to become better versions of themselves.

QUEENISM

If you see something, say something!

Most of the time, people handle formal professional development better than they receive informal professional development. They might interpret informal professional development – like being pulled aside and gently corrected – as criticism and rebuke. However, don't let this deter you. They might not appreciate your taking the time to challenge them to do better in the moment, but eventually, they will see the value of it. They will realize that you were only challenging them to be better and do better. Some of the most positive feedback I've ever received about professional development came after I retired. Someone sent me a picture of herself in a new educational leadership position after she'd received a promotion. There was also a note enclosed thanking me for always pulling her aside and being direct with her, for pushing her, for expecting the best out of her, and for believing in her when other people, including her teachers, didn't believe in her. Another individual, a principal I once supervised, reached out to me and said something similar. She said, "I understand now. At first, I thought how you were challenging me and what you were asking of me was a bit much, but now, I understand!" It might take people a while to realize that your coaching and correction is only your effort to lift them as you lead them, but they'll get there. Never stop lifting through professional development. The better your people look, the better you look as a leader. When they come out looking and sounding like better versions of themselves in the workplace, everyone wins, including the kids.

When you lift through professional development, you are lifting your team of leaders to greatness without them even knowing it. You're pouring into them personally and professionally and leading them in such a way that they will make an even bigger difference in the lives of the kids. However, as you are professionally developing others, be sure that you are also continually developing yourself. If you're giving advice to lift others through professional development but not engaged in development yourself, the people you're trying to lift will not be as receptive to what you are saying to them. When you schedule formal professional development sessions, if you expect the teachers to stay, you can't be running out of the school door at three o'clock or sitting in your office while they are sitting in a development session. You, as the educational leader, should participate in these sessions, too! Further, you don't need to sit at the back of the room like someone who is observing while "the people who need it most" are learning; you need to be in the middle of the group, raising your hand, asking questions, and actively participating in the professional development to show that you value what is being taught. Lifting through professional development is important, but if you keep disappearing, setting a doctor's appointment, or coming up with "good reasons" to be absent every time professional development is scheduled, your staff members are going to begin to wonder. They are sure to think that either your timing is off, or you – their leader – are determined not to learn anything new. Thus, if you are going to lift through professional development, you've got to model the value of it.

Third, motivation helps to lift people as you lead them. However, motivating others cannot be done according to a one-size-fits-all technique. You can't just say, "This is how I'm going to motivate all of my teachers at once, and if they don't like it, oh well. You can't please everybody." No, you've got to meet people where they are. You must motivate them in ways that are most effective in moving them as individuals. Sure, this takes more work than a broad-brush approach to motivation, but you want to be effective, don't you? Well, being an effective leader takes going the extra mile and putting in the extra work. Do some investigating to find out what motivates the individuals you lead. What makes them feel special, valued, cared for and appreciated the most? Do they like notes in their inbox? Do they like for you to drop by their classroom or office to chat with them? Do they like you to praise them in front of all the other team members? Do they like little thoughtful gifts? Do they like food? Let me pause on this one and tell you something you might have already discovered: *everybody* likes food, and I mean *everybody*! I've never met a team of people that wasn't motivated by food.

Finally, acknowledgement and appreciation help to lift the people you lead. There is not a person alive who does not like to be acknowledged and appreciated. People will say, "Oh, no need to say, 'Thank you!'" or "You didn't have to go through all of that trouble for me!" but they're usually just being modest. Not only do they desire it as much as everyone else does, but they need it. It's human nature to crave acknowledgement and appreciation. You can meet this need in your team of leaders in several ways.

One of the most popular ways that I acknowledge and appreciate our staff in school is through appreciation days. I'm sure you've heard of National Teacher Appreciation Week. No educational leader who wants to be viewed as an effective leader can miss out on this week. You've got to maximize every day of this special week for teachers. They look forward to it all year as a celebration for all of the hard work, dedication, time, energy, and sacrifices they invest into ensuring their students get a quality education. As a principal, I spent a lot of money on Teacher Appreciation Week. I would go all out. I would change the teacher's lounge into a day spa, and then I would ask them to stay an extra hour or so after school to go over some data. Then, when they showed up for the meeting in the lounge, they would see the spa and get so excited that they were about to get a pampering session! There would be relaxing chairs, nice soft music, cool cucumbers to place on their eyes, and professionals there to give them hand massages. I would also host theme days with lots of food for them in the teacher's lounge, not only during Teacher Appreciation Week (during which I included paraprofessionals, custodians, and other essential staff, because they are very important as well) but throughout the year. I've learned a not-so-secret secret to making most people feel appreciated: feed them.

Everybody loves food! Regardless of what type of appreciation, event, or meeting you host for your staff, if you have food for them, that's gold! At every faculty meeting, I made sure there was food. When I need to review some data with my team members, I would say, "Let's sit over some coffee and donuts and look over the data." Any time we did a professional development workshop or seminar, there was food. There's just something about having food present that makes people feel like they're not really in a meeting or work seminar. One year, when I was a principal, I did a book study called "A Recipe for Great Teaching." Every team at the school had to present a chapter and bring their favorite recipe. We were eating *good* every month! There's a reason why some food is referred to as "comfort food." Food has the ability to bring a great deal of comfort to any setting. It makes work not feel like work. It transforms environments from being formal and stuffy to being casual and fun. Food can even soften the blow when it's time to have difficult conversations. Rather than feeling like you're a supervisor who is about to call your team members to the carpet, it feels more like sitting around and eating with your family. I refer to it as "talking about tough stuff at the table," and I did it often as a leader.

There were other small yet significant ways that I showed my appreciation for my staff, and I didn't have to break the bank to make them happen. Instead, I was resourceful. Most of what I did was either free or cost very little. In addition to using my discretionary fund, I would ask people for gift cards to appreciate my staff. I had business owners who partnered with the school and provided donations and freebies. These efforts cost me a little extra energy but didn't cost me much money. Therefore, appreciating my staff in tangible ways was doable.

Then, there were the intangibles; I would use every opportunity I could think of to lift them in ways that they couldn't touch but that they could feel. Sometimes, it would be writing nice notes to teachers after I did a walkthrough. Other times, it would be giving the cafeteria workers a thumbs up when the lunch was on point. There were also times when I would ride the floor buffer so my custodians could take a break. Not only did these things lift my staff but it modeled for them more that we were all on the same team. There are no big Is and little yous in the school-house; we're in different positions but we're all equally important. My actions spoke much more loudly than my words ever could to convey such a message. You can't just Lead and Lift in words; you have to show it through your actions. An act of lifting is an act of love!

During my years as a director of schools, if I was on my way to visit your school, I might stop and pick up a sausage biscuit for the principal. Handing the bag to him or her, I would say, "Hey! Let's have something to eat first before we get into these streets and see what these children are learning!" I always jokingly referred to the school hallways as "the streets." Then, once we got into "the streets," I would call all the teachers by name and ask them how their babies were doing. I didn't just ask questions like this and keep moving; I stood there and actually waited for a response. Remember our conversation on the work of an educational leader being Heartwork? This is Heartwork. When I left, everyone I had encountered at the school was glad to have encountered me that day. They loved to see me in their hallways.

I think it was because I gave them a sense that I wasn't there to lord over them; I was there in the trenches with them.

I know for a fact that my acknowledgement of everyone I worked with helped to increase my leadership effectiveness. I didn't acknowledge them as a superior looking down on people whom I thought were in an inferior position. I acknowledged them from a "Let's do this together" perspective. Whether in person or over the phone, when I'm talking to people I lead, I'm not talking "to" them; I am talking "with" them. In fact, one of the nicest things that people have said to me was that they appreciated how even though I was their supervisor, they felt like we were in it together. I was there to put up decorations and wipe down tables. I was there to help clean up after an event and make copies for a teacher. I was there to sit by a principal's side when she needed to have a difficult conversation with a teacher. I was there to be a sub when a principal needed to take a sick kid to the doctor. I genuinely wanted to be there for the people I led, and their appreciation for my being there showed through the lengths they were willing to go to in order to produce good work for the children.

I also lifted my staff through appreciation just by being there to step in for them. I've already told you about how, as a director of schools, I would step in for the principals. Whether they needed me to step in so they could get into their classrooms and do observations, shake hands and kiss babies, or go to their children's events during the workday, I was there for them. I would always say to them, "You lead, and I'm going to be there." They always knew that there was one person they could call to give them whatever support they needed, and I was glad to be that person.

Faculty members are not the only ones who need leading and lifting; custodial personnel do, too, as they are essential to the culture and climate of the school. Although I used a weekly custodial checklist with my custodial team, they were also celebrated with wonderful surprises during the holidays or when teachers were lifted. While you are leading and lifting your staff, you will need to encourage them to, in turn, Lead and Lift the students they serve. You will need them to become champions for all of the students they interact with in the building each day. If you Lead and Lift your staff so that they can turn around and Lead and Lift the students but they don't Lead and Lift the students, the work that you do to Lead and Lift the staff is in vain.

The late Rita Pierson, my role model, once said, "Every child deserves a champion. An adult who will never give up on them, who understands the power of connection, and who insists that they become the best they can possibly be." I could not agree with her more. To be a champion for children requires that we lead with them in mind at all times. We must analyze data and drill down to root causes. We must come early and stay late. We must learn about their out-of-school environments and how they impact the students' school environment. We must listen to their voices. In order to lift the whole child, we have to understand the whole child and everything that contributes to who they are.

Lead and Lift requires that we ask more of our teachers, administrative staff, counselors, custodians and all who come into contact with them. We don't just ask them to lead; we also ask them to lift. However, they won't be equipped to lift the children until we model for them how to lift. As a principal, I did my part to lift students as much as I could. Whether it was attending student games or events and cheering them on, throwing a party to celebrate student achievement, having a Student of the Month luncheon, or tutoring students personally, I stepped in at every opportunity to lift them.

Typically, the teachers carry the bulk of the load in lifting the students because they spend so much time with them. They can lift students as they need them by employing many of the same approaches their building leader or supervisor used to Lead and Lift them. In any case, they cannot just stand in front of the classroom, lecture the kids, say, "I expect for you to get this done," and call it a day. There must be some lifting in the classroom along with the leading – some inspiration, motivation, incentivizing, acknowledgements and appreciation.

I once had a leader who told me that he believed that kids should be intrinsically motivated and that educators shouldn't have to provide motivation, awards and incentives to get them to do what they were already supposed to do in the classroom. Of course, I disagreed and emphasized the importance of lifting the kids. Eventually, he learned. As quiet as it's kept, this leader was not alone in this belief; I know that a lot of educators believe this as well – they are just not bold enough to say it aloud. However, as they continue in their educational career, they will learn that lifting students is essential to the students' performance. It's not just a desire; it's a need.

Lifting is especially important in low-SES schools where dropout rates are often higher than average. For a number of reasons, many times, the kids just don't go to school. When they do show up, the teacher cannot lead the classroom by saying, "You need to come to school every day. If you don't start coming to school every day, the police are going to knock on your door and take your parents to jail. You're supposed to come to school, so do it! Now, everyone, take out your textbooks." How well do you think those kids will perform in their academics with being led without being lifted by their teacher? Not well. Think about it. If children live in a place where they don't feel safe at night and then go to school and don't feel safe or cared for, there's no way they are going to perform well. They need their educational leaders to make them feel special. They need their teachers to inspire, motivate, support, incentivize and reward them. Otherwise, they will ask themselves, "Why do I need to do well here?" When they can't come up with a good answer, it won't even make sense to them to go to school at all. Therefore, I encourage educational leaders to put in the work necessary to balance leading and lifting. In the end, every stakeholder in the school benefits from it, and we all win!

(7)

LOVE AND EXPECTATION

You can't be an effective leader without love. You may hold the title and position of leader, and you might even be able to move people to accomplish tasks and fulfill their duties, but remember: effective leaders are those who can influence people to get things done and feel good about it. If people you're leading get things done but don't feel good about it, you'll be leading, but you'll never be as effective as you could be. People will always hold something back from you. They won't give you their all. Unless, that is, you show them love.

The Love and Expectation principle is a simple concept: love everybody and expect the best out of them. You might say, "Oh, that's easy to do. I'm naturally a loving person, and I look for everybody to do their best just like I do my best." I know the concept is a simple concept to understand, but when it comes to putting it into practice, it's not that simple.

It's easy to love people when they're doing the right thing, following the rules, cooperating, and not causing you any problems.

However, as a leader, you're going to find that there are a lot of people who fall outside of these parameters. They don't always do the right thing. They don't always follow the rules. They are uncooperative and cause you a lot of problems. Can you still love them, or will you withhold your love and resent them instead? Will you still encourage them and challenge them to be their best, or will you just bide your time with them and let them be as mediocre as they want to be until you don't have to deal with them anymore? See, it's easy to love loveable people; it's harder to love the unlovable. That's where the work begins. That's where this conversation about Love and Expectation needs to be had.

Then, there's expectation. You can't say that you love those whom you lead in an educational setting and not have high expectations of them. Expectations go hand in hand with love in the field of education. The reason behind this is clear: if you don't expect kids to do, they won't do. They won't operate with "can." Instead, the learning atmosphere will be a chaotic free-for-all. All of the kids who fall under your leadership need to feel that you love them, and because you love them, you expect them to be their very best. This is another one of those things that is not just a desire; it's a need. Kids need to feel loved, hear their names called, be respected rather than denigrated, and made to feel capable of being the extraordinary young people they are. This is a principle that I have never settled on or compromised about in my tenure as an educator. It is non-negotiable.

Anyone who has worked with me over the years will tell you that if you are going to work under my supervision as an educator, operating based on Love and Expectation is a prerequisite. It represents the foundation for how the teachers will relate to the students. If a teacher does not love the students and expect the best from them, they will not give their very best to their children every day – this is something else that I require. There have been occasions when I have observed leaders and teachers not giving their best to the students and asked them what was going on with them. Often, they will say that they are having personal problems, or that they are having problems at home. I understand that things happen, but even these are not reasons to justify not giving the students their best.

I've always told those under my supervision, "Don't bring your baggage to the school day!" There's no way you can lead with Love and Expectation when you are distracted by your own personal problems, so it's best to leave these things at the front door. If you had a fight with your husband, leave it at the door, because the children in the school building are counting on your undivided love and attention that day. If your children aren't acting right at home, call and tell me and say, "Hey, I need an hour. Can you please get me some coverage?" If an hour is not enough, take a mental health day. Whatever you do, leave anything that is going to prevent the kids from feeling your wholehearted Love and Expectation outside.

Love is not just an emotion you feel; it is an action you show. No teacher can tell me, "I love my students," but not take necessary action to demonstrate that love when it is needed. For example, during my principal years, if I was doing a walk through and passed by a classroom where I saw a student with his head down, I stopped. My first thought would be, *Why is this teacher still standing there teaching the class when this student has his head down on his desk?* For the teacher to continue teaching without caring that the student had his head down suggested to me that she hadn't placed any expectations of the student. In other words, she might be thinking, *If he wants to lay his head down and not learn, that's up to him. I have a classroom of students to teach. I'm not going to force him to sit up and learn.* This mentality reflects neither love nor expectation.

What I would expect from the teacher is that she stops teaching and have enough love for the student to be concerned about him. Ask him why his head is down. Is he sick? Send him to the nurse's office. Is he hungry? Get him something to eat. No child can be asked to learn if his basic needs are not being met (and if you think that this is not your problem to address as an educator, you need to go back to the Heartwork chapter). If the child is neither sick nor hungry, the teacher needs to clearly set the expectation: "I expect you to sit up, listen and do the work." If the student does not comply, that's when it's time to take action by asking someone from the office to come and talk to him. However, by no means is it acceptable for a teacher to keep teaching while a student has his head down in the classroom in her full view. Teachers must lead their classrooms with Love and Expectation!

The principle of leading with Love and Expectation is particularly important when dealing with students of color, primarily Black boys. Many educators view Black boys as being difficult students, as problems that they would rather not deal with in the classroom. If they could speak openly on their feelings about Black boys, they would tell you that these boys don't listen, they talk back, they are lazy, they are disruptive, they are disrespectful, and they don't want to be in the classroom or do the work. The same educators will also confess that they are often scared of these boys, because they are intimidating because of the aggression they might display. This is why when the Black boys are not behaving as they should in the classroom, the teachers are more likely to ignore them rather than confront them; they don't want a scene. The teachers know that they can't just go through and put all of the Black boys out of their classroom, so they let them stay in the room but provide the minimal amount of attention possible to these boys. It's not uncommon to walk by a classroom and see that the students who have their heads laid on their desks or who are clearly disengaged from the rest of the class like they are on their own little island – and who are being ignored by the teachers – are Black boys. I know what they are thinking about those students: *If you give me a hard time, fine... I'll just let you sleep until class is over and I don't have to deal with you anymore. You'll be another teacher's problem in about an hour.*

As an educator who truly has a heart for children – all children, not just the easy ones – letting a child sleep through class is never okay. It screams, "I have no expectations of you in my class because I do not love you and do not care whether you succeed in life or not!" If I observe this happening in a classroom, I ask if I can talk to the teacher for a second and ask her why the kid has his head down or why the kid is allowed to be disengaged and on his own island. I use it as a teachable moment – a moment for professional development – about loving the students enough to expect more of them. The principle of Love and Expectation says, "I love you too much to not let you do any work."

As a leader, you have to learn to love unlovable kids and still expect them to do their very best. You must learn to love unlovable teachers and expect them to give it their all. A lot of times, as a principal, I encountered teachers who didn't show certain kids – the more difficult, less compliant ones – love. As a result, the teachers didn't build a relationship with these kids or expect the kids to do what they asked them to do. As soon as they asked these kids to do something, it was already in their mind that the kids weren't going to do it. Guess what? Kids pick up on this. They know when you love them, they know when you believe in them, and they know when you expect the worst from them, even when you say with your lips that you expect the best. Kids are deeply perceptive and very smart, despite how hard of a time they might give you to make you think otherwise.

Students are not the only stakeholders worthy of love in the organization; every stakeholder who is a part of your organization deserves your love as a leader. It comes with the territory of being an effective leader. As the leader, your teachers have to feel your love, your administrative staff has to feel your love – everyone has to feel your love. Some leaders might say, "But Dr. McQueen, I'm not really an emotional person. I'm good with getting things done and telling people what to do, but I'm not good at the whole 'love' part. I wouldn't know where to begin." My response to this is that you can't give to others what you haven't experienced, been taught or seen modeled before you. Some people might have experienced traumas that their supervisors will never know anything about, and this trauma has blocked their ability to communicate or demonstrate love. This is why it's every building leader's responsibility to model what love looks like for the people they lead. That way, if the people under their supervision have never experienced or been taught how to show love, there's no excuse; there's a living, breathing model in action right before them to show them how it's done.

You can't say that you love someone without showing this love through some form of relationship. In fact, it is love that bonds people together in a relationship. It doesn't have to be the deep kind of relationship where you talk to each other and spend a lot of time with each other every day. It can be the kind of relationship in which we never say anything more to each other than "Good morning! How are you doing today?" or make eye contact and smile when you pass one another in the hallway, and yet, you just know that there is a loving relationship there. As a principal, the students in my school knew that I genuinely loved them. I didn't get to talk to each one of them every day, but when I saw them, I would greet them, and when they had an issue, I was there for them. They were never on their own – never alone. They knew that they had a principal who cared for them, had their best interests at heart, and was willing to do and give whatever necessary to ensure that they had what they needed to succeed in school and in life. They had an advocate in me, a leader who was looking out for them, and to them, this was a genuine demonstration of love.

I've found that building relationships with stakeholders is by far the most effective way to move them to get things done. You know and I know that it's human nature to do things the easiest way possible. If you leave it up to them, people will take shortcuts, not invest the time and energy needed to produce the best quality, and water down their efforts on the way to getting things done. However, if you place expectations on people to do things based on a certain standard, they will exert themselves to a greater extent, investing more time, energy and effort than they naturally would on their own to meet your expectations. This is especially true if they know you love them. When people know you really love them, they will go to the ends of the earth to not disappoint you and your expectations of them. Love brings out the best in us!

We build relationships to show love to our stakeholders, and once they know we love them, they will give us permission to challenge them with expectations beyond what they ever thought possible to achieve. For example, as a principal, one year, I showed love for each of my teachers on Valentine's Day. These were the same teachers that challenged with the highest of expectations day in and day out, so they deserved to feel some love on this special day. The day before Valentine's Day, I ordered two dozen long-stemmed roses and picked them up on the way to school the next morning. After the morning announcements, I put the roses on a cart and made my rounds. I went by every classroom to hand deliver them to each and every teacher in front of their class. I just popped in and said to the class, "Good morning, class." They replied, "Good morning, Dr. McQueen!" Then, I turned to the teacher, handed him or her a rose, and said, "During your break today, take some time to smell the roses. Kids, give your teacher a round of applause for being such a wonderful teacher!" Then, all the kids would clap, cheer and shout, "Yayyyy!" Kids love to cheer on their teachers. Even the meanest teachers in the building seemed to be floored by this gesture. It was my hope that my showing them this small act of my love for them was chipping away at anything inside of them that was keeping them from showing love.

Now, I don't know what they did with those roses. A lot of the teachers stopped by my office at the end of the school day to say, "Thank you," because they felt loved and appreciated on Valentine's Day. Some of them might have hated my guts and thrown their rose in the trash can, but that was not going to stop me from giving them that rose! Those who didn't love me back would never be able to say that they didn't love me because they never received acts of love and kindness from me. Some people, you're just not going to reach. It's our responsibility as leaders to show love to our stakeholders, regardless of how they feel about us. We cannot control how our stakeholders on the other end of it receive it.

As the building leader, you can also show love through making concessions that make your staff members' jobs a little more comfortable. For example, the dress code for the school I led as a principal was business casual; I wanted the teachers and leader to wear slacks and a blouse or dressy top to work because I wanted the kids in the school to be able to look at these models and see a picture of where they were headed in the future. As you probably already know as an educational leader, teachers love wearing jeans. Jeans are like gold! At one point, my teachers asked me if they could wear jeans every Friday. After giving it some careful thought, I decided that I could make this concession; as an act of love and care for them, I modified the dress code for the month if they paid their PTA dues.

The first time I saw my staff wearing jeans on a Friday... oh my *goodness*! I was not used to that at *all*! Part of me bristled at seeing them walking around looking so casual in what I had always tried to represent as a "professional" environment. However, I got used to it, because it made the teachers so happy. It boosted their morale, increased the positive energy in the school, and made everyone more relaxed. I was fine with this as long as their work did not relax along with the dress code. In fact, instead of every Friday, I allowed teachers to wear jeans every day during the month of May because that was the time of standardized testing. I said to myself, "I need these teachers to make these kids successful, and if it takes wearing jeans to school, so be it!"

After I made this change to the teachers' dress code, I vividly remember one of my friends, who was a principal from another school, calling me and saying, "You set me up, McQueen! My teachers heard about how your teachers get to wear jeans to work, and now they're putting the pressure on me to make the same change. You set me up!" I just laughed and said, "I didn't set you up. Your teachers set you up!" In the end, making that slight change in the dress code cost me nothing, but it meant everything to the teachers I supervised. They felt the love that I had for them in making that decision, because it was not something that other schools in the district would have done. Because of the love they felt from me and my consideration of them, they gave everything they had to make those kids successful so that I, their leader, could shine. This, among many other acts of love that I did for my staff, never escaped the attention of everyone in my building. I know this for a fact, because my successor, someone who had moved up through the ranks as a teacher and had become principal there, used to call me. The teachers would talk about the different things I had done for them and apparently, they expected the same of her!

Just as high as your love is, you, the building leader, must keep your expectations of those under your supervision higher. Publish a clear record of your expectations for all of your staff and hold them accountable for them. For example, as a principal, I had an expectation that my teachers arrive at school on time. I considered this a practical and reasonable expectation for a professional educational environment, as well as a necessary one because it modeled for the kids the importance of timeliness. However, I had this one teacher who kept showing up late to work. She wasn't super late; she was usually only about seven minutes late, but it was every day. One day, after she kept showing up late, I was standing at her room door waiting for her when she arrived at the school. She was actually the best teacher in the building, so I almost hated having to say something to her. However, you have to have the same expectations for everyone and show the same love. I said, "Hey! How are you doing this morning? Stop by my office later and let's have some coffee."

Once she got to my office later that morning, I held her accountable to my expectation of timeliness. It was a necessary meeting, because I couldn't tell the other teachers to meet my expectation of arriving to work on time and not say anything to her when this teacher repeatedly arrived late. I wasn't mean to her; you can hold people accountable without being mean to them. When she arrived, I said, "Let me ask you a question. I notice that you've been coming to work about seven minutes late. You're coming from Louisa, right? Are you using I-64 to get here?" She said, "Yes." I said, "The traffic on that road during that time is really heavy. Why don't you come I-295 instead? That alone is going to take seven minutes off of your drive so you can get to work on time!" She replied, "Sure. Okay!" After that, she actually started getting to work 45 minutes early! She wanted me to know that she understood the expectation and was determined to rise to it! The point was made that we have an expectation that our teachers are timely in their arrival. The teacher would go on to share this story with everyone in the building, and before long, everyone knew that Dr. McQueen had the same high expectations of everyone at the school.

No environment can be excellent without high expectations, and no leader can be effective without placing high expectations on those who are under his or her supervision. However, as necessary as high expectations are in the educational environment, people will resist rising to meet them every step of the way. The teachers might believe that the expectations that the building leader has on them are too high and that the expectations they are asked to place on the kids are too high, because the kids are not capable of rising to meet them. Building leaders might believe that the expectations their school directors place on them for the school are too high; they have too much to do already and there's no time to do the extra that is needed to meet all of the director's expectations.

Striving to meet high expectations can put pressure on a person to perform well and zap the fun out of the work or task at hand. High expectations make things less comfortable for those who are challenged to meet them, because extra effort must be exerted in order to successfully rise to them. A person can't be lazy and meet high expectations. People don't like being pushed and challenged to get to their next level. This is why the people you lead will kick, fight and scream each time you place high expectations on them. However, if you are going to increase your leadership effectiveness, you must maintain your high expectations of those under every level of your leadership. The reason:

students are depending on everyone in the building meeting those high expectations. I always say to my staff, "I'm always going to set the bar high, and if you don't reach it, I can lower it. But I'm not going to lower it before you even try to reach the bar!"

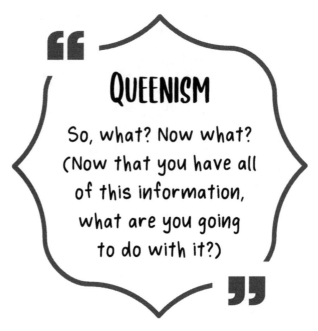

QUEENISM

So, what? Now what? (Now that you have all of this information, what are you going to do with it?)

Finally, never let your preconceived notions about how people will react to your high expectations stop you from implementing them. Yes, sometimes, people will moan and groan about your high expectations, but other times, people will surprise you with how open they are to rising to your expectations. For example, I remember receiving a phone call from a principal who needed some advice. She wanted to do some trainings for her teachers for a few days before school began, but she was apprehensive about asking them. She thought that they might give her some pushback about having to do the trainings before the school year officially began, even though they would be paid for the time it took to participate in them. I said to her, "You shouldn't approach this with the presumption that they are going to say, 'No.' Don't count them out before you ask them. Besides, who is going to say 'No' to a little pocket change?" Sure enough, she asked them, and they said, "Of course!" She called me back all excited that they had said "Yes" to the trainings. They were more than eager to participate in the trainings and had no ill-will towards her for scheduling them in the days leading up to the start of school. This small victory made the principal want to do even more out of the box things in her school; it gave her confidence to set a high bar among her workers. If you are going to increase your leadership effectiveness, you must do the same: set the bar high, and expect that people are going to want to rise to it!

Ultimately, the high expectations that you have of people, from students, to teachers and administrators, will challenge them to be their absolute best. When you lead people from the heart, prioritize their needs before paper, help them to discover a better way through having them help you understand, trust them fully and verify as a safeguard, keep the needs of children first, and lift people as you lead them along the journey, you will indeed be an effective leader in education. Objectives will be accomplished, lives will be forever changed, people will be forever grateful for your leadership, and your name will forever be mentioned in the stories of those whose lives you have touched along the way. It's not rocket science! It's all about love and expectations, but the greatest of these is love.

I would like to thank every person who helped to shape my leadership identity and wish you all great success on your educational leadership journey! – Q

"QUEENISMS"

"When you change the language, you change the culture!"

"You're not going to make a paycheck on the backs of these kids!"

"Let data drive your decisions. Behind every set of numbers is a story waiting to be told. Every data point points to a child's needs."

"Stand and deliver! Sometimes, you have to stand up and say the tough things that people don't want to hear."

"Whether it's a good or bad decision or a successful or unsuccessful program, everything points back to the leader who writes, nurtures, and rolls out the vision!"

"You won't need to do damage control if you do your due diligence!"

"Leadership is the invisible rope that pulls other people to greatness. They don't even know they are being pulled!"

"I love teachers, and I love kids more!"

"We don't teach content; we teach children!"

"Don't hire fast. Hire well!"

"There is an art and a science to leadership."

"If you see something, say something!"

"So, what? Now what? (Now that you have all of this information, what are you going to do with it?)"

About the Author

During her career as a professional educator, Reverend Dr. Michelle Kelly McQueen-Williams has shown a deep concern for the educational, social, and emotional well-being of the children she has encountered as a teacher, assistant principal, and elementary principal for Henrico County Public schools. She was named the first principal of Harvie Elementary, the 45th elementary school to be opened in Eastern Henrico County. Dr. McQueen-Williams recently retired as the Director of Elementary Education in Henrico County Public Schools. She currently serves as Executive Director of P-12 experiences and educational initiatives at her alma mater, Virginia Union University.

McQueen-Williams is a product of the Richmond Public School System and holds a Bachelor of Arts degree in Journalism from Virginia Union University (where she was crowned Miss Virginia Union University), a Master's and a Ph.D. in Educational Leadership from Virginia Commonwealth University, and a certificate of completion from Virginia Tech's Aspiring Superintendent's program. Dr. McQueen-Williams graduated with honors from the Samuel Dewitt Proctor School of Theology at Virginia Union University with her Master of Divinity and is now matriculating through the Doctor of Ministry program there.

Licensed and ordained, McQueen-Williams currently serves as an Associate Minister at the First Baptist Church of South Richmond, where the Reverend Drs. Dwight C. and Derik E. Jones are the pastors. Civic minded, she seeks to motivate, empower, and inspire all with whom she comes in contact.

Made in the USA
Columbia, SC
30 January 2021